GUNSMOKE

John W. Sheehan Jr.

Motorbooks International
Publishers & Wholesalers ®

First published in 1990 by Motorbooks International Publishers & Wholesalers, P O Box 2, 729 Prospect Avenue, Osceola, WI 54020 USA

Motorbooks International books are also available at discounts in bulk quantity for industrial or sales-promotional use. For details write to Special Sales Manager at the Publisher's address

Library of Congress Cataloging-in-Publication Data
Sheehan, John W.
    Gunsmoke / John W. Sheehan, Jr.
      p.   cm.
    ISBN 0-87938-446-8
    1. USAF Worldwide Fighter Gunnery Meet, Nev.—Pictorial Works.
    2. Nellis Air Force Base (Nev.)—Pictorial works. I. Title.
UG703.S47 1990   90-33859
623.7′461′0222—dc20   CIP

Printed and bound in Hong Kong

To my parents, John and Nelta Sheehan, of Kerrville, Texas

This book would not have been possible without the assistance and support of a great many people. Many thanks to the men and women of the Gunsmoke teams; Capt. Tom Christie, head of the Gunsmoke Public Affairs staff; TSgt. Shiela Amos of the 188th TFG, Arkansas ANG; John Hoffman of the National Guard Bureau Public Affairs office; the Public Relations offices at LTV and General Dynamics; Greg Field, editor at Motorbooks International; Sharon O'Donnell, manuscript editor; and Colonel Whit Swain, USAF (Ret), former F-4 driver who reviewed the manuscript.

I owe a special debt to Ian Francis for his ability to see in black and white and capture the action on film.

Although many people were involved in producing this book, the final decision about its contents was mine and so is the responsibility for any errors or omissions.

John Sheehan
Fairborn, Ohio

On the frontispiece: An F-16 sits on the Gunsmoke ramp awaiting a Profile III mission. It is carrying an inert Mk 82 500 lb. bomb on each wing. Note the shark's teeth motif in grease pencil on this Mk 82. *John Sheehan*

On the title page: These F-4Es from the 3rd TFW, Clark AFB, Philippines, stand ready for the day's competition at Gunsmoke 1989. *Ian Francis*

On the front cover: A pair of F-16s from the Montana Air National Guard. *Jim Benson*

On the back cover: The Gunsmoke '89 patch shows the four major Gunsmoke aircraft: the F-4 Phantom II, the A-7 Corsair II, the A-10 Thunderbolt II and the F-16 Falcon.

Contents

Chapter 1

Introduction

Gunsmoke! The word that, for many people, conjures a vision of US Marshall Matt Dillon staring steely-eyed down a dusty Dodge City street, a steady right hand poised over his well-worn Colt forty-five, anticipating the inevitable move from his opponent that will start a chain of events leading to one of their deaths.

That was television, and the marshall never lost a gunfight. Today's Gunsmoke is a contest of another sort, where the six-shooter has been replaced by a rotary cannon and the opponent is a scoring system, a videotape replay and the relentless pressure of competition. This is practice, a simulation or an exercise, call it what you will, where there are no "bad guys" and no one returns fire or launches deadly surface-to-air missiles as the seconds tick by on the long run into the target. Having said that, Gunsmoke remains a true test of the ability of the US Air Force's tactical aircraft and their aircrews to do what counts—put bombs and bullets onto the target.

Held biennially (every two years for us civilians), Gunsmoke brings together the best of the Tactical Air Forces' air-to-ground units for what is officially known as the USAF Worldwide Fighter Gunnery Meet. It is hosted by the Tactical Fighter Weapons Center at Nellis AFB, Las Vegas, Nevada, and sponsored by the Tactical Air Command (TAC). At Gunsmoke, the competition pits teams from units in the continental United States (CONUS) as well as overseas against one another for a fourteen-day extravaganza of flying, bombing and strafing, weapons loading and aircraft maintenance events. When the smoke clears, the "air-to-mud" community will have selected an overall Top Gun, the best gunfighter in the tactical aviation business. In addition, an overall winning team at the meet will have been chosen, as well as individual team winners in each category. The level of competition and the prestige associated with it are evident in the comments of the competitors:

In the words of one competitor: "Everyone in the fighter business aspires to be a member of one of these teams. It's one of the ultimate things you can do as a fighter pilot in your weapons system because the selection is so difficult."

Another pilot added, "It stays with you for years—who was on which team, when, and what they did."

Chapter 2

History

The current Gunsmoke competition has its roots in a long line of tactical fighter air-to-ground weapons meets held at Nellis AFB, the "Home of the Fighter Pilot," at least as far as the US Air Force is concerned. Now as then, the purpose of the competition is to demonstrate the capabilities of USAF tactical fighters and their crews under realistic conditions, and to display a variety of weapons delivery techniques best suited to tactical scenarios. The present-day Gunsmoke events also call for demonstrations of skill from aircraft maintenance and weapons loading teams.

The first weapons meet was held at Nellis in 1949, hosted as it is today by the Fighter Weapons School (FWS). Both piston-engined and jet-powered aircraft competed, and the overall winner was the team from the Fighter Weapons School. The FWS team repeated its win in 1950 for the USAF Gunnery Meet II, the last meeting of jet- and piston-powered aircraft. The Korean conflict intervened for the next three years and tactical fighter pilots were engaged in a true test of their skills, taking the fight to the enemy under actual wartime conditions. After the Korean armistice, Tactical Air Command (TAC) returned to the weapons meets at Nellis, this time as an all-jet contest. The 1954 meet, renamed the USAF Fighter Weapons and Gunnery Meet III, was held on Nellis Range 1 and included teams from Tactical Air Command (TAC), the Far East Air Force (FEAF), Alaskan Air Command (AAC), Air National Guard (ANG), North East Air Command (NEAC), US Air Forces Europe (USAFE), Air Training Command (ATC) and the Strategic Air Command (SAC). In addition to these day-fighter teams, this competition also hosted for the first time nuclear strike teams from SAC, TAC, USAFE and the FEAF—all flying Republic F-84 Thunderjets. The Nellis FWS team, flying for ATC, was the winner once again.

The 1955 weapons meet was unique in several respects: it was the debut of the Loadeo competition for the teams' weapons loading crews, and the first competition to see the 20 mm cannon carried on the North American Aviation F-86Hs flown by the USAFE team. Gunnery Meet IV hosted eleven teams from across the Air Force, with each team comprised of six pilots and twenty-five airmen. The contest also saw the first non-USAF team member, Marine Corps major George Dodenhoff, assigned to the 21st Fighter Bomber Wing (FBW) team flying F-86Fs. The 1955 event was the initial performance of the Republic F-84F in competition, and marked another first when an aircraft from the 140th Fighter Interceptor Wing (FIW) was hit on the range by a ricocheting bullet which damaged its engine. The winners? No surprise, the Nellis team.

Gunnery Meet V, in 1956, saw the Nellis team take its fourth straight win in the day-fighter category, with the USAFE team winning the special weapons delivery events. This competition also included seven shows by the USAF Thunderbirds at Nellis and in Yuma, Arizona. Flying for the 50th FBW team, based at Toul-Rosieres, France, was Lt. Col. Chuck Yeager.

A revision of the concept behind the weapons meet brought with it a new name, William Tell, in 1958. Now, the day-fighters would compete in air-to-ground events at Nellis, while newly introduced interceptor aircraft would fly their missions at Tyndall AFB, Florida. This was the first all-supersonic meet, with the Nellis team once again taking home the honors in most of the events. This World-wide Tactical Fighter Weapons Meet VI was also the venue for demonstrations of some of the USAF's latest weaponry. The F-100C and F-104B put on flying demonstrations, as did the F-105 which made several supersonic passes. An F-104 fired the recently developed GAR-8, later redesignated the AIM-9, Sidewinder missile. Other demonstrations included precision flying by the Thunderbirds and the Minutemen of the Colorado ANG, inflight refueling, and an F-100D zero length launch. Subsequent changes included the move to a biennial format, and the use of more realistic targets such as pyramid towers and the "dart" for air-to-air gunnery. The Loadeo portion of the meet now included nuclear weapons loading, and the competition was rescheduled from June to October, which brought some relief from the intense heat of the early summer months in both Florida and Nevada.

More changes were in store at the 1960 competition, where conventional weapons events included close air support, interdiction and air-to-air categories. The nuclear weapons dive-bombing event was replaced by over-the-shoulder, retarded and laydown nuclear delivery techniques. TAC's Lockheed F-104 Starfighter, flown by the team from George AFB, California, competed for the first time. This meet also included the first live television cov-erage of the competition. Overcoming the odds, the Nellis team took home the trophy again, making this their sixth straight victory. Contest officials reacted predictably, bar-ring Nellis from any further weapons meets; the constant training, superior pilots and excellent weapons ranges available at Nellis were considered an unfair advantage over the other teams.

Two years later the William Tell meet had evolved into perhaps the most realistic of any up to that point. The team concept was scrapped, with one primary and one alternate pilot permitted from each fighter wing, and all weather aircraft were added to the roster of competitors. The year 1962 marked the sole appearance of the Repub-lic F-105 Thunderchief in competition. Realism was

An F-51 Mustang takeoff during the first Air Force Gunnery Meet at Nellis AFB in 1949. This meet had piston engined and jet powered aircraft competing on an equal basis. USAF photo- graphic collection, National Air & Space Museum, Smithsonian Institution

An F-80 Shooting Star pulls up after completing a strafing pass during the second Air Force Gunnery Meet, 29 March to 4 April 1950, at Nellis AFB. (USAF photographic collection, National Air & Space Museum, Smithsonian Institution)

An F-84 Thunderjet pilot releases his practice bomb during the first Air Force Gunnery Meet, held at Nellis AFB from 4 to 7 May 1949. This low-level pass makes the current Gunsmoke altitude restric- tions look pretty conservative. Note the extended ventral speed-brake. USAF photographic collection, National Air & Space Museum, Smithsonian Institution

enhanced by ten reconnaissance sorties flown by McDonnell RF-101 Voodoos to provide target information for subsequent weapons deliveries by other teams. Some target folders were provided to aircrews as little as three hours before required engine start times, and the air-to-air crews found themselves losing points if more than one pass was required to destroy the target or if it was partially destroyed.

Another Asian conflict was in full swing by 1964 and it would be another seventeen years until the gunnery meets were resurrected. TAC did conduct some smaller tactical exercises such as Coronet Sharpshooter at Nellis and Gila Bend, Arizona. William Tell continued at Tyndall AFB every two years as a strictly air-to-air competition.

Gunsmoke was back in 1981, complete with the full team concept used at previous meets. Events included air-to-ground deliveries, navigation-attack, weapons loading and aircraft maintenance.

USAF aircraft had advanced two generations since the last Gunsmoke competition. In 1981, competing teams flew the F-4, A-7 and A-10 aircraft. Two years later, F-16s were on hand for the first time and have been the airplane to beat from that year on. The Top Guns for the 1983, 1985, 1987 and 1989 meets were all flying the Electric Jet, and the dominance of the F-16 shows no sign of slacking.

A closer look at the aircraft flown during Gunsmoke reveals the reasons for the distinct advantage the F-16 enjoys on the bombing range:

The elder statesman of the quartet is the McDonnell F-4 Phantom II. While the original naval version was flown in 1958, the first model of the Phantom selected for US Air Force service, the F-4C, was not flying until 1964 and carried no internal gun. This model, along with its similar F-4D cousin and the later F-4G Wild Weasel variant, is forced to use an external gun pod for strafing missions. The definitive version of the Phantom II, the F-4E, comes equipped with an internal 20 mm cannon and the solid state AN/APQ-120 radar. In spite of a certain amount of success in the hands of US and Israeli aircrews, the F-4 bombing system is relatively old and

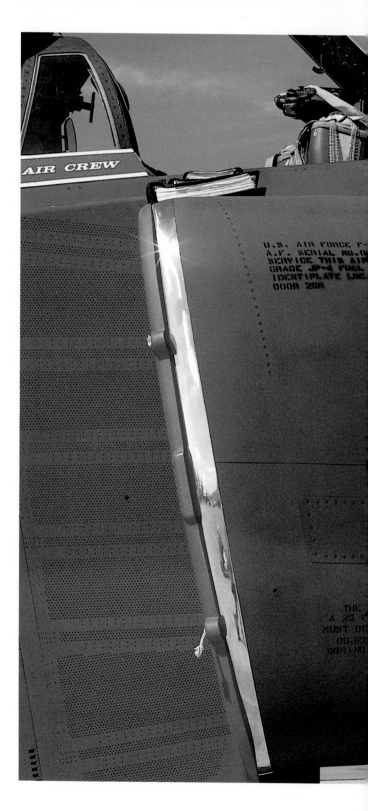

The bright red "Razorback" logo and red trim under the canopies stand out from the gray and greens of the European I camouflage scheme on this F-4C from the 1985 Gunsmoke team of the 188th TFG, Fort Smith, Arkansas. The 188th has since converted to the F-16 and retired their Rhinos, which included the high-time aircraft in the USAF F-4 fleet. John Sheehan

PACAF

KUNSAN AB

AF 81
WP 7 14

uses a mechanical computer to produce weapons release information.

Next on the roster is the Vought A-7D, the Corsair II. Derived in large part from the F-8 naval fighter, the A-7 was designed to replace the aging Douglas A-4 as the US Navy's primary carrier-based attack aircraft. After a first flight in 1965, the A-7 was then selected for the US Air Force and a dedicated version, the A-7D, was flying by 1968. The key to the A-7's nav-attack system is the ASN-91 computer, which takes information from an inertial navigation set, a doppler unit and the APQ-126 radar and integrates it to provide all navigation information, as well as automatic guidance to a selected target and necessary weapons release signals. The A-7 carries the standard M61 internal 20 mm Gatling gun cannon.

The third Gunsmoke competitor is the Fairchild Republic A-10A Thunderbolt II (an appellation unknown anywhere but in US Air Force press releases), reverently referred to as the Warthog or Thunderhog. Built solely for the ground attack role, the A-10 was flown initially in 1972 and, after a flyoff against the competing Northrop A-9, was selected for production to replace the A-7. Designed around the General Electric GAU-8/A Avenger 30 mm rotary cannon, the A-10 is a flying gun platform with an impressive weapons carrying capacity. Unfortunately, its avionics equipment falls short of that required for a modern attack aircraft to be successful in the A-10's intended operating area, the Central European theater. Basically a "point and shoot" airplane, the A-10 is equipped with a Kaiser head up display (HUD) and a dual-reticle optical sight which can be used with the Pave Penny external laser-tracking pod. The A-10 is a simple, reliable airplane or, as one of its pilots explains, "It's basically a '57 Buick with a gun in it."

As a relative latecomer to Gunsmoke, the General Dynamics F-16 Fighting Falcon dramatically demonstrates the increased capability provided by a computer-driven flight control and nav-attack combination. Flying for the first time in 1974 as the GD model 401, the Electric Jet, or the Viper, has matured into the free world's most capable fighter aircraft, equally at home in the air-to-air, air-to-ground or nuclear strike role. Equipped with a Westinghouse APG-66 radar set and a Sperry air data computer, the F-16 features a completely fly-by-wire con-

No way to mistake these F-16s for any but those assigned to the "Wolfpack" of the 8th TFW, Kunsan AB, Republic of Korea. The standard "WP" tail code has been replaced by the stylized wolf's head and two color trim, moving down to the bottom of the vertical fin for the duration of the Gunsmoke meet. John Sheehan

13

trol system and fully integrated computer-directed weapons release capability. Whether on a strafing run using its 6,000 round per minute 20 mm rotary cannon or releasing iron bombs from a pop-up delivery, the F-16 displays consistent accuracy that makes it the airplane to beat at Gunsmoke, whether flown by active duty, Air National Guard or Air Force Reserve pilots.

One mainstay of the tactical fighter force is absent, however, from the list of Gunsmoke competitors. The General Dynamics F-111, known unofficially as the Ardvaark, has never been a participant in a Gunsmoke meet. While there is no doubt that the F-111's main mission is air-to-ground, it's the lack of an installed gun system that bars this extremely capable all-weather strike aircraft from showing its stuff. That's unfortunate, because the F-111 crews are masters of warp speed on the deck delivery modes required to survive on the modern battlefield.

A view of a 185th TFG A-7D showing the customized intake covers used during Gunsmoke 1985. John Sheehan

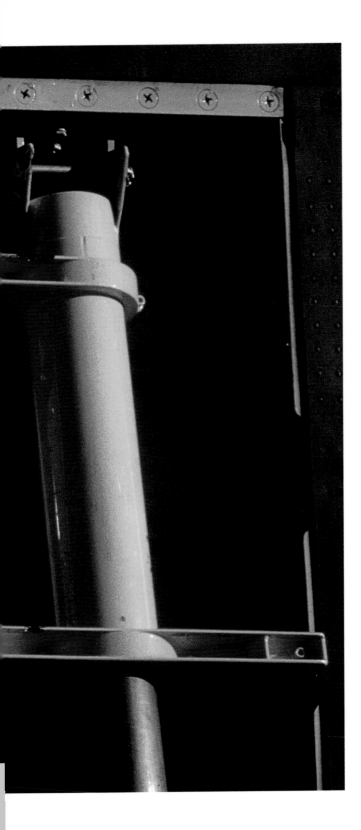

Not all the unofficial nose art is on the nose. Pop open the boarding ladder door of an A–10A Warthog and you may find anything; on this 81st TFW bird from RAF Bentwaters, England, it's the Warthog himself, toting a GAU–8 30 mm cannon and an AGM–45 Maverick missile.

17

A–10As of the 23rd TFW, England AFB, Louisiana, getting their
last chance inspection prior to takeoff at Nellis. The 23rd's shark-
nose paint scheme was earned by the wing's forerunners, the Flying
Tigers of the American Volunteer Group, while flying P–40s for the
Chinese prior to the US entry into the Second World War.

Another touch of color on the A–10As from Louisiana—fin markings representing the three squadrons assigned to the 23rd TFW. John Sheehan

next page
A–10As from the 343rd TFW sported tail codes outlined in white, the Alaskan Air Command emblem, and blue fin flashes complete with fox logo. John Sheehan

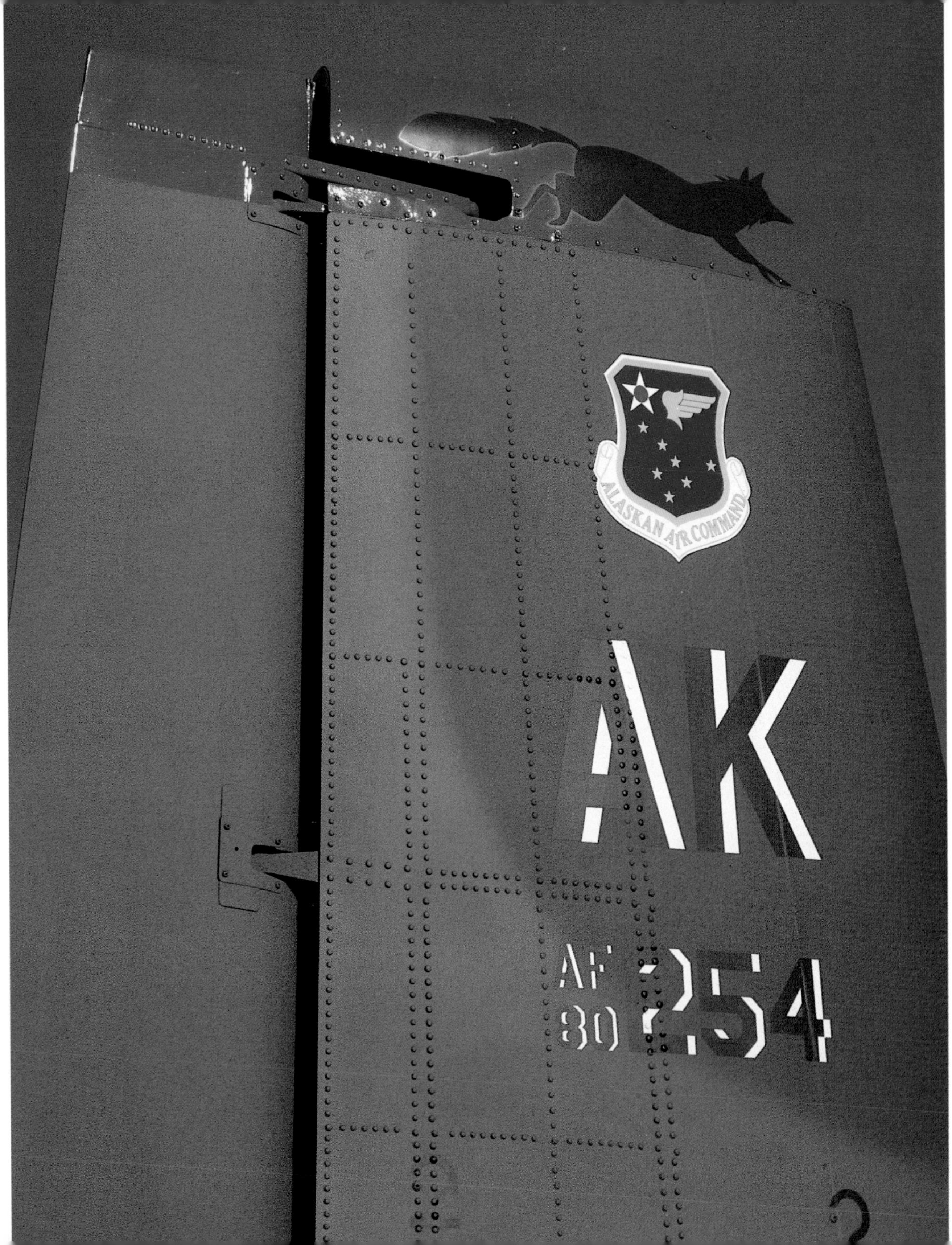
ALASKAN AIR COMMAND
AK
AF
80
254

22

The tail of a 388th TFW F-16 is framed against an American flag during the final awards ceremony of Gunsmoke 87 at Nellis AFB. The 388th was named top team for that event. SSgt. David Nolan, AAVS

Chapter 3

Training to Win

Preparation for the Gunsmoke meet begins anywhere from three to six months prior to the October date set for the opening day. The amount of time and resources devoted to working up to the meet depend on the additional taskings each unit may have to fulfill, as well as the importance given to Gunsmoke by each unit commander. In recent years, some units have started their preparations

Shoulder patch of a 181st TFG crew member. The 181st is based at Hullman Field, Terre Haute, Indiana, and has been associated for years with Indianapolis and the 500, as reflected in the checkered flag motif complete with F-4 and Indy car designs. John Sheehan

as little as one month ahead of the meet, selecting the aircraft and personnel based on availability and practicing as hard as possible in the few weeks left to them. Other units, with full support from commanders, select their teams and aircraft as far ahead as six months and use the team approach, separating the Gunsmoke crews and aircraft from normal unit flying activities. In these organizations, the Gunsmoke team has priority for flying hours and range time, while the ground and aircrews are freed of routine duties to devote their efforts solely to preparation for Gunsmoke. This latter approach appears to have had the most success in producing winning Gunsmoke teams.

The Air National Guard and Air Force Reserve teams have to contend with the fact that their members have, for the most part, full-time civilian jobs that allow them to participate in Gunsmoke practice events on weekends only. Very few employers are willing to let someone take time off for a Guard or Reserve job that doesn't make their company any money. As a result, these teams practice when they can and try to get as much from each training session as possible. As one ANG unit advisor put it:

"We're going to have one full timer on our Gunsmoke team—the rest are airline pilots working a full time job. We don't have the assets that some of the other teams can dedicate to Gunsmoke. We can't shut the squadron down to fly just one set of people and airplanes. We're glad to go to Gunsmoke—we may learn something. It allows the team to get into their system better, learn more, and improve their performance. We don't put as much into it as other units, so our cost to learning ratio will be higher.

"The team has been through inspections and competitions before; they've made their mistakes previously. In the three weeks left prior to Gunsmoke we'll be working three or four days a week getting ready. After we return, we've got six months of preparation for an upcoming Operational Readiness Inspection (ORI), with our runway scheduled to be closed during a portion of that time. When we plan, we work in years where the active duty units work in months. Six months equates to 12 days of training time for us."

Selecting teams

Each team is selected to participate in Gunsmoke in a different way. One F-16 unit from the Air National Guard was picked to compete simply because other Guard F-16 outfits were still in conversion status and had other commitments. The A-7 Guard units, on the other hand, took part in a shootout to determine which ones would go to Gunsmoke. While some teams must practice on their home turf, others are lucky enough to have some training time in areas that closely resemble the Nellis range complex.

The selection of team members varies from unit to unit, but with the majority of the Gunsmoke competitors it boiled down to going through aircrew records, scouring the list of available pilots (and F-4 WSOs) for the best on the base. Although flying skills certainly played a part in the selection process, each team member was also judged on his experience, participation in previous Gunsmoke meets and his ability to stay cool under stress.

Maintenance team members first of all had to be volunteers (or at least someone who wouldn't object too strongly when "volunteered") who were selected by their supervisors as the best qualified for the team. Here again, selection was based primarily on performance, but attitude, experience in previous competitions and the demonstrated quality of grace under pressure were major factors in selection for the team.

Each unit participating in Gunsmoke is looking for a winning team and, from experience, they realize that putting such a team together is an art, not a science. Skill, test scores and job knowledge all count, but even more important is the ability to think on your feet, remain calm when things seem to be falling apart, and to be a team player for the entire stress-filled fourteen days of a Gunsmoke competition. Finding the right combination of professional abilities, personalities and desire among the thousands of people assigned to a Tactical Fighter Wing isn't easy, but then that's what makes it a competition and not just another training exercise.

Preparation

TAC's Ninth Air Force sent its F-16 and A-10 teams to Gunpowder, a mini-Gunsmoke competition held at Mountain Home AFB in Idaho to prepare the crews for the high and dry conditions at Nellis. One of the pilots explained: "This wasn't done in 1987 and the 9AF teams didn't do well. This year the 9AF commander revived the idea and its a real confidence builder. It turns out that these ranges are not much different than our home ranges."

This F-4E is ready for practice bomb loading on the pylon-mounted triple ejector rack (TER). It also carries, on the pylon shoulder stations above the TER, launcher rails for two AIM-9 missiles. The long lens protruding from the leading edge of the wing is the heart of the Target Identification System, Electro Optical (TISEO), installed to give F-4 crews greater visual identification capability than the Mk 1, Mod 0 eyeball. John Sheehan

The team composition varies from unit to unit as well. The active duty teams are normally much younger than their Guard and Reserve counterparts, but they are made up of only the very best a wing can supply. Even in a large wing such as the 81st Tactical Fighter Wing (TFW) from RAF Bentwaters, England, only the top five pilots are going to be picked for the Gunsmoke team. A second A-10 team was made up with three graduates from the USAF Fighter Weapons School at Nellis on board—a real bonus in knowledge of tactical delivery techniques and familiarity with the Nellis ranges.

In the months prior to the actual meet, ground crews will test and tweak each jet until it flies just as its pilot wants; if an aircraft can't be brought up to a pilot's standards, it is exchanged for another aircraft and the entire process starts over. During this early phase of preparation, pilots will fly their range training missions in each aircraft available to the team, getting a feel for the jets and working on the decision to select one over another. Toward the end of the training phase, the pilots will select one aircraft to complete their training sorties and fly during Gunsmoke events. While the maintenance crews work as hard as they can to optimize each airplane's performance, the pilots can spot the minor differences among the jets and choose to stay with an airplane that gives them the best results.

Weapons load crews train tirelessly during this period, putting in twelve hours or more a day, a pace that is as hard on their families as on the crew members themselves. Time after time, the same six bombs will be loaded under the watchful eyes of senior NCOs, always looking for a way to cut a few seconds off of the overall time. As hard as the loaders are training, other maintenance specialists are working equally long hours going over each system on the team's aircraft, trying to wring from them that last little bit of extra performance that may mean the difference between winning or losing a given event. During the final days prior to the competition, aircraft are repainted as needed, although it appears that they all were due for scheduled "corrosion control" a few days before Gunsmoke begins. While nonstandard paint schemes are not encouraged, a close look inside an A-10 boarding ladder door or at the top of a vertical fin shows that the long-standing tradition of personalizing Air Force aircraft is far from dead.

As October approaches, some of the teams leave their home stations and deploy for a week or two to one of the

A-10As from the 23rd TFW team, with specially made Gunsmoke engine intake covers. The "Flying Tiger" on the wing's emblem can be seen on the second aircraft. John Sheehan

bases that can provide conditions similar to those that will be found at Nellis. For crews from the Midwest or the East Coast, a couple of weeks to practice flying from Luke (Arizona) or George (California) AFB can really hone their skills and gives them much needed time to adjust to flying in a high desert environment. The new location also provides time for the jets to dry out in the low western humidity, and for onboard systems to stabilize in the desert air. With practice flights completed, it's time for the team to pack their bags and head for Nellis on the first weekend in October.

The competition

Crews competing in the current Gunsmoke meets know that they are up against not only some of the most aggressive and well-trained opponents they're ever likely to run across, but also the most demanding set of rules and scenarios designed to test their flying skills to the limit. Starting with day one, when every team is assigned a designated arrival time and the difference between winning and losing is measured in seconds as the teams are clocked past the Nellis tower, the meet progresses to the business of delivering munitions on target—on time.

After some initial practice runs to get a feel for flying the Nellis range complex, each team is scrutinized as they make their runs on each of three delivery profiles:

Profile I Each team flies two four-ship missions to hit the target from a basic box pattern. Every team member makes two passes in three different delivery approaches, a

The unique tail codes and markings applied to F-4Es from the 3rd TFW, Clark AFB, Republic of the Philippines. The diagonal strip running through the tail code is an electroluminescent panel which can be used during night formation flying to reduce the aircraft's visibility. Ian Francis

30 degree dive, a 20 degree low-angle low-drag, and a 10 degree low-angle high-drag. After the bombing runs are complete, each team moves to the strafing range where they are scored based on firing a total of 100 rounds per aircraft.

Profile II Next comes the tactical profile where each team is required to fly two four-ship missions delivering weapons from a pop-up pattern as well as a level bomb release. Each team makes two passes for each of the two delivery modes, and they are scored based on possible exposure to enemy fire during the pop-up and the accuracy of their deliveries. Strafing passes for this profile are flown from a box pattern.

The 185th TFG from the Iowa ANG managed to dress up their Corsair IIs for Gunsmoke, complete with the bat logo added to the two-tone gray camouflage. John Sheehan

Close-up view of a New Mexico Air National Guard A–7D with the Zia (sunburst) and roadrunner, carrying a bomb in each claw. John Sheehan

29

Profile III Acknowledged as the toughest part of the meet, this section calls for the teams to fly two-ship navigation-attack missions covering anywhere from 150 to 200 miles. The crews do not know the route in advance; prior to takeoff, they are provided with map coordinates which correspond to mandatory checkpoints along the route. Each checkpoint is marked with orange panels on the ground. To score, one of the two aircraft must pass between the panels within five seconds of their predetermined time. The crew then has one pass at the target; scores are determined by miss distances and deviation from scheduled bomb impact times.

After their aircraft return from the daily mission, each team's weapons loading crew is judged on their skill in weapons loading during an integrated combat turnaround, or ICT, scenario. This involves taking an aircraft returning from a simulated combat mission, reloading it with designated weapons, and having it ready for its next mission in the minimum amount of time consistent with required technical procedures and safety factors.

During the entire competition, aircraft maintenance personnel assigned to each team are observed as they prepare their aircraft for each mission, accomplish necessary maintenance and follow mandatory technical and safety procedures.

Customized engine intake covers on this Air Force Reserve A-10A from the 930th TFG, Grissom AFB, Indiana. John Sheehan

next page
This F-16 from the 388th TFW, Hill AFB, Utah, has been dressed up for Gunsmoke. A tricolor tail flash and white outline for the tail code add some color to the Falcon's low-visibility gray camouflage. The addition of the 388th's logo has forced the serial number normally carried in the middle of the vertical fin to be added toward the bottom in minute lettering. John Sheehan

Chapter 4

Welcome to the Home of the Fighter Pilot

Once every two years, the constant stream of activity at Nellis AFB, Las Vegas, Nevada, home of the USAF Tactical Fighter Weapons Center, dies down and the flightline is relatively empty. The Red Flag competitors are gone, and it will be weeks until the next "flag" exercise is due. The south end of the parking ramp is empty, providing an almost unobstructed view of the casinos and hotels on the Las Vegas strip, six miles away. For some, those locations offer the only game in town; however, for a very special group of people at Nellis, the first two weeks in October will demand their total concentration and efforts while they take part in Gunsmoke, the Tactical Air Force's competition to select the Top Gun and Top Team in the air-to-ground business.

Arrival time

That first Sunday starts early for the ground crews and the operations and maintenance judges, who have arrived days before each team's aircraft. The competition at Gunsmoke is fierce, and the judging begins before the first set of wheels thumps down on the Nellis runway. Each team has been assigned an arrival time, and they will be clocked as they pass abreast of the Nellis control tower on the east side of the runway.

As the first arrival time approaches, the ground crews are on the ramp setting up each aircraft parking spot with fire bottles, aircraft ladders, tool boxes and wheel chocks. Not a bomb has been dropped, but there's no doubt that the contest is on. The maintenance crews are wearing standard-issue utility uniforms, the ubiquitous BDU (battle dress uniform), but these are the tailored and pressed variety, fresh out of the clothing sales store via some long hours behind a sewing machine and ironing board. Each member of a Gunsmoke team is judged on military dress and appearance, and it shows. As the crews ready their parking spots, they are looking good and they know it. The old heads on the teams realize that this gives each person that extra sense of confidence that is absolutely vital to winning Gunsmoke.

As the magic hour approaches, the tempo of activity on the ramp dies down; each spot is ready with a crew chief standing at parade rest, hatless in the October Nevada sun. Off to the north, if you've got good eyes, the first set of aircraft reveal themselves as five black specks against the light blue sky. Watching the clock and air speed, the teams

The Gunsmoke patch, worn (legally) only during the competition at Nellis. The heart of the meet is contained in the patch, with cross-hairs superimposed over a bull's-eye surrounded by the four competing aircraft types. John Sheehan

aim for their preassigned "time on target" as they flash past the Nellis tower. Each team is videotaped and timed to one thousandth of a second. Gunsmoke is officially on and the five aircraft in each team enter the Nellis pattern out of a tactical break over the field.

Each team is given a scheduled arrival time when they must be 500 feet above the runway, with at least three of the team's aircraft in echelon formation, abeam of the Nellis tower. As the team arrives in the local area, the lead pilot checks in with Nellis Control and is given holding instructions and a time hack from the Gunsmoke judge assigned to the tower. Nellis Control stacks each team in order at the holding point; at a predetermined time, a team will be cleared to depart the holding point, calling in as they make their initial approach to Nellis Runway 21.

It's a simple time and distance calculation exercise when figuring the air speed required to arrive dead on time; however, the winds, clock accuracy and plain luck have a lot to do with deciding which team will take the arrival competition. The lead pilot of the team that arrived 2.948 seconds after their scheduled time, or fifteenth out of the sixteen teams, explained:

"Well, we could have done a lot better, but I got something in my eye, and I couldn't see well enough to get an accurate update on my computer. And then traffic control came up on frequency and said that I had to give the password to get clearance to pass by the tower, but nobody told me the password, plus I didn't get enough advance per diem to last the whole deployment, and besides, Mom always liked you best."

The teams that have made the long overwater flights from European or Pacific bases, some as long as 6,500 miles, have been in the States for a few weeks honing their skills at other weapons ranges. Teams located in the United States may have also been working out of another base closer to Nellis in the weeks prior to the meet, while others not so fortunate will have to make a single run from their home station. In either case, the teams will all fly to a holding point nearby Nellis, orbiting until they are released for their run to the base.

One team, flying their twenty-one-year-old F-4Es out of Indiana, was forced into an early Sunday morning takeoff and flying a single 1,500 mile hop to Nellis simply because some of their "weekenders" couldn't get to the field before Saturday night. Two of the team pilots who fly for major airlines during the week put their suitcases on a plane headed for Las Vegas from Dallas, and then caught a flight to Indiana (they were eventually reunited with their

F-16s of the 423rd TFW, Misawa AB, Japan, on the Gunsmoke ramp prior to crew arrival. Ian Francis

uniforms at Nellis). After all of that, the team officially arrived five seconds past the appointed time, the result of waiting too late to push the power up on the run to Nellis from their holding point.

If being just shy of three seconds late puts your team in fifteenth place, what does it take for a winning time? In this particular event, the winning team blasted by the Nellis tower a mere 0.202 seconds off of their assigned time!

After landing, they trundle down the taxiway to the Gunsmoke ramp and head slowly for their parking spots. Each crew is primed and ready to marshal his or her bird into the spot with precise, well-rehearsed movements that would do credit to the Thunderbirds. Like clockwork, each aircraft pivots smartly and rolls into its assigned spot as the crew chief's hands raise overhead and cross at the wrists, signaling the pilot to brake the airplane.

The five members of an F-16 team discuss a little strategy on the ramp at Nellis. Ian Francis

An updated A-7D from the Sioux City, Iowa, Guard. The Euro I camouflage has been replaced by the ubiquitous two-tone gray scheme. New intake covers were made for the 1989 meet, with the bat deleted in favor of a simple "Sioux City" and an Indian headdress, which symbolizes the Indian warriors who once roamed the Iowa plains. John Sheehan

Welcome to Gunsmoke

The rest of the ground crew move toward the aircraft, chock the main gear, connect the ground cable and, as the canopy moves up, install the aircraft ladder. The crew chief is ready to assist by taking the pilot's helmet bag and handing out the first welcome to Gunsmoke. As the pilots and crew chiefs postflight their planes, the Gunsmoke maintenance judges move in, watching the activity and looking for any lapse in established maintenance procedures. They examine each set of aircraft forms, peer into wheelwells and access panels and look for the slightest sign of shoddy work or malfunctioning equipment. They don't find any, and for the next two weeks they will con-

tinue to search without much success, if any. These aircraft were picked for Gunsmoke weeks, and in some cases months, in advance and they've received the most intensive care they can get in a tactical flying unit. All airplanes leak and all airplanes have minor mechanical problems—that's the nature of the flying business. Come to Gunsmoke, though, and you'll see just what a handful of dedicated and psyched-up professionals can do. For two weeks, these aircraft are tweaked, tuned, polished and shined to within an inch of their lives. Gunsmoke may be a bombing and gunnery competition first, but the maintenance folks are big players in the overall team standings and they know it. It shows in their dress, in the determined look on their faces and in their controlled rush to keep their aircraft looking sharp.

That first burst of activity during the team arrivals is the precursor of many hours of hard work ahead as the teams move into the main events for the Gunsmoke competition. The unofficial slogan for the meet is "the best of the best," and the level of competition among the teams backs that up. You don't get to Gunsmoke without being good, and you don't win unless you're better than the best of your competitors on each day of the meet. No one event can win the Gunsmoke for you, but a bad performance in one event can certainly lose it. The level of competition has increased to a point where nearly perfect performance is demanded in every event, and the difference between winning and coming in second is often measured in single-digit scores.

As the first round of Profile I flights approach, the pressure on the individual aircrew members mounts. Practice is one thing, and all the players have shown that they can hack it during the weeks of preparation. The time for learning is over; every bomb counts on the range and there are no opportunities to refly a bad pass. It's time to see who has what it takes and who doesn't.

A few minutes spent with any of the teams soon reveals that this is a unique gathering—every one of the best fighter pilots (and F-4 Weapons Systems Officers, or WSOs) in the Air Force have managed to show up at Nellis at the same time! Quite a coincidence. There's no argument that a fighter pilot without an ego is like a shark without teeth. What's striking about the teams at Gunsmoke is not that the egos are there, but they've taken a back seat to the needs of the teams. Each pilot is out to give it his best shot and take the coveted Top Gun award, but not at the expense of losing the team competition. The team members review videotapes of each pass after each event is flown; the critiques are characterized, as they say, by frank and open discussion. A bad bomb is a bad bomb, and no one says otherwise. Usually it's the pilot who is his own worst critic. The team members watch the tapes

This F-16 team knows that the competition starts well before the aircraft turn a wheel. Crew chiefs are standing tall as their pilots check the forms and then step out smartly on their way to the cockpit. Gunsmoke demands this level of dedication and attention to detail from each team day after day as the meet progresses. Ian Francis

36

repeatedly, analyzing air speed, dive angle, pipper placement and other indicators to find the problem and offer suggestions for improvements that will garner more points on the upcoming flights. It ain't over 'til it's over, as they say, and one bad score can be overcome by a series of good passes the next day. The whole attitude of each team is to start out going full blast and not let up until the last pass is scored.

Each team is housed in a small office on the second floor of the Red Flag building near the Gunsmoke ramp. It's cramped quarters for the five pilots, video equipment, planning tables and assorted pieces of equipment and personal gear. Throw in another five WSOs for the F-4 teams and now you're talking *really* close quarters. For the next two weeks of activity, this room will be the hub of each team's activity as they plan for upcoming flights, review previous range tapes and cope with a steady stream of media people wanting a piece of their already full schedule to ask the time-honored question, "What's it like out there?" The team members are remarkably tolerant of this parade of outsiders, at all times the epitome of the Air Force professional while they respond over and over to some fairly obvious questions that yes, Gunsmoke *is* worth all the time and the money the Air Force is spending on it because it provides valuable training in the techniques that would be used in a tactical battle, and demonstrates the capabilities of the front line aircraft in the Air Force inventory. Hidden behind those words is the fact that it's also a hell of a lot of fun!

During the day, the ramp temperature at Nellis can rise to over 100 degrees Fahrenheit but falls rapidly once the sun drops behind the city lights and casinos of Las Vegas. Overnight lows may reach the thirties, so that by the time maintenance crews are on the ramp in the morning the summer weight BDU uniform with rolled sleeves makes for pretty chilly working conditions. As the sky behind the Sunrise Mountains, to the east of the field, begins to lighten, ground crews are swarming over their team aircraft in preparation for the day's mission.

Traditionally, each separate specialist works his or her own particular area and no other, but not at Gunsmoke. The entire maintenance team is out early, formed up line abreast for a FOD (foreign object damage) walk on their portion of the ramp, searching for any stray piece of wire or a misplaced fastener that could cut the tire of a taxying aircraft or be sucked into an engine intake and turn several million dollars worth of rapidly rotating high-temperature steel into an unusable piece of scrap. As early as the ground crews are out, their everpresent shadows, the judges, are there too, distinct among the camouflaged team members in their more formal, blue uniforms, complete with red badges and the dreaded clipboard. As the

aircraft are prepared for each flight, every maintenance action is scrutinized and any oversight mercilessly recorded, resulting in the loss of points in the overall scoring process.

Each aircraft is checked for fluid levels, tire pressure, electrical problems and myriad other functions essential to a flawless flight. While the maintenance crews work, armament systems specialists examine the munitions loaded on the aircraft one final time to verify the integrity of the system.

Gunsmoke is no place for a hung bomb or inadvertent release; either of those malfunctions could end any team's chance of taking home the trophy. For the basic weapons delivery and tactical bomb delivery events, each aircraft will carry six 25 lb. BDU 33 practice bombs which duplicate the ballistics of full-size iron bombs, as well as 100 rounds of TP (target practice) ammunition for their strafing passes. The navigation/attack sorties are flown carrying two inert Mk 82 500 lb. bombs fitted with BSU 49 Air Inflated Retarder (AIR) devices. Each team brings a single weapons loading crew which must perform daily munitions loading for each flying event as well as compete in the two separate munitions loading events. Consequently, these team members are under constant pressure to perform while being tracked by both maintenance and munitions judges—quite an exposure to competition for some of the first-time team members.

As engine start time approaches, the aircrew members are dropped off at the team location and begin their preflight activities. All five of the team's aircraft are prepared for each mission, up to and including engine start. The spare pilot will remain in the cockpit with engine running until all four of the primary team members have radioed that they are good for this flight, at which point the engine will be shut down. Each pilot will begin his walkaround with his aircraft crew chief, starting on the left side of the plane and working his way toward the rear of the fuselage and back up the right side, around the nose and back to the starting point. Everything that the maintenance specialists had previously checked and verified will be rechecked and reverified—you can't have too many pairs of eyes looking for problem areas with this level of competition. Other specialists stay close, ready to answer questions or correct any minor difficulty noticed by the pilot.

Nothing else draws a crowd like the launch of a group of fighters, and while the team members work their aircraft, a "gathering of eagles" is slowly forming on the sidelines. Wing, Group and Squadron commanders, Ops Officers and various high rollers assigned to the Gunsmoke staff are on hand to observe; they can't resist the call of the flightline. One by one they gather in the area of the first teams to launch, watching the activity and discussing the morning's missions. Chief Judges are there as well, watching the watchers and doing their best to remain inscrutable and avoid giving away the answers to the oblique questions thrown their way, such as: "How's it going?"; "What does it look like so far?" Those team members not actually involved in the launch also huddle on the sidelines, giving encouragement and trying to cut the tension with a few suggestions shouted to the participants. In some cases, family members have traveled to Nellis to be with their teams and at times seem to outnumber the uniformed members of the crowd. There's something slightly incongruous about groups of children, wives, husbands, fathers and mothers and significant others, all dressed in their best Las Vegas outfits, watching these green and gray fighters go off to simulate bombing someone into oblivion.

Preflights complete, the crews clamber into their cockpits, dragging up helmet bags full of navigation charts and other fighter pilot paraphernalia. Their helmets sit on canopy rails, waiting for their owners to don the nylon liner that covers their heads and gives some relief from the hot spots caused by the heavy and ungainly helmets. Crew chiefs assist with strapping in and connecting the communication and oxygen lines and then scramble down the ladders to connect their ground intercom headsets, complete with the "Mickey Mouse" earphones. Other team

With its pilot's helmet sitting ready on the canopy sill, this F-16 is cocked for the morning range mission. A Gunsmoke emblem has been placed on the visor cover of the otherwise drab gray helmet, below which is the name of the aircraft's dedicated crew chief. Ian Francis

members take down aircraft ladders and make final checks of the "-60" (dash sixty) power carts used to start each aircraft. As the second hand ticks, the power carts are started, their internal turbines spinning up until the noise level reaches a painful whine. Those in the crowd without ear protection move back or poke an index finger into each ear, while others closer to the aircraft put on their ear defenders or take out the small, yellow foam cylinders supplied like bubble gum on every flightline, rolling them up until they fit snugly into the ear. This cuts the noise back to an acceptable level and makes conversation possible, providing you're nose to nose with the other party and are also an accomplished lip reader.

Just as the noise level stabilizes, the flight leader signals for engine start, and all five aircraft fire up. Everyone takes a few more steps back and anyone standing directly in front of the aircraft is sharply reminded by a crew chief that there are better places to be. With power on the aircraft, standing in front of a loaded 20 or 30 mm cannon is not a wise move.

The avionics available on each type of aircraft has a lot to do with determining how far in advance of takeoff engines are started. The older F-4s and the A-10s, with fairly basic systems, require very little lead time prior to moving out of the chocks. The F-16, on the other hand, needs some fifteen minutes of power on time to stabilize

This F-16 pilot on the 432nd TFW team from Misawa AB, Japan, is fired up and ready to go. He flashes a traditional thumbs-up as he moves his Falcon toward the taxiway enroute to the quick-check area at the end of the runway. Ian Francis

and align the inertial navigation system (INS), which can then provide precise navigational information to the pilots. It is absolutely critical that this system be operating properly, which includes feeding in the exact latitude and longitude of the aircraft as it sits in the chocks. Armed with that information, the F-16 INS can navigate its way to the target and return to base with only a few feet of error at the mission's end.

Other crews flying older aircraft are not so fortunate; for them, navigation is still labor intensive and heavily dependent on the skill and experience of the pilot. The F-4 has a slight advantage in this area since it carries a second crew member, the WSO, in the rear seat who is dedicated to navigating the aircraft while the pilot only has to fly where he's told to (if you're imprudent enough to believe that, keep it to yourself while in the vicinity of the Phantom drivers). The A-10 has been characterized by its pilots as having a T-LAR system for bombing and navigation, T-LAR as in "That looks about right"!

Once the aircraft engines are started, the -60 power carts are shut down and disconnected and each jet is on internal power. Any pieces of stray equipment are moved away from the aircraft's taxi path and, as the pilot lifts both hands in a fist with thumbs pointing outboard, specialists crouch down and duckwalk under the wings, grab the ropes on each set of wheel chocks, then scramble back out from under the aircraft, pulling the chocks with them. The crew chief makes a last check with the pilot over the ground intercom, unplugs it from the intercom jack and returns to the nose of the aircraft. As the team leader signals his intent to taxi, the crew chief raises both arms to the vertical and motions the aircraft toward him, as if trying to pull the plane from its resting position. As the pilot slowly advances the throttle, the whine of the engine increases and the wheels begin to move forward, gradually at first and then more rapidly as the throttle advances. Objects to the rear of the aircraft shimmer in the heat of the engine's exhaust, and the overwhelming sensation is one of noise and that special smell of JP-4 fumes that permeates everything on the flightline. It may not be chemically addictive, but once you've smelled it you can't pass up the chance to stand in it again.

The aircraft is rolling now, bouncing slightly on its landing gear struts as it passes over tar strips on the ramp. The crew chief motions the pilot forward until the nosewheel is on the yellow taxi stripe painted on the tarmac, and then drops an arm, pointing the pilot toward the main taxiway. The nosewheel turns, responding to the pressure of the pilot's feet on the rudder pedals and the nose of the aircraft swings in an arc past the crew chief who comes to attention and snaps off a perfect salute to his departing teammate and receives an emphatic thumbs-up from the pilot in return. One by one the other three aircraft on the team repeat this sequence, taxying out, following the leader down to the main taxiway, past the spare aircraft at the end of the row. In most cases, a wing or squadron commander is waiting at the end of the line, showing the flag and exchanging raised thumbs with each of his pilots as they roll past. He and everyone else on the team has done all they can do; it's up to the aircrews now to go out and do the job that Gunsmoke is all about—put bombs and bullets on the target.

The four team aircraft move down the taxiway, passing other competitors going through the same preflight drill, past the F-16s, A-10s and F-15s assigned to the Fighter Weapons School, and then the blue and white F-16s of the Thunderbirds. At the end of the taxiway they move into the quick-check area for a last chance inspection. Each ship is marshaled into position, chocked and given a rapid but thorough onceover by maintenance and armament troops, observed, as always, by the judges. Satisfied that each aircraft is ready for flight, the ground crew pulls the safety pins and devices attached to the practice bombs and the triple ejector racks (TERs) on each wing. Chocks are then pulled and the team aircraft roll into position at the end of the runway. A few minutes wait, and then throttles are shoved forward, brakes released and the jets move down the runway, gathering speed until they gradually lift into the air and begin their turns to form up on the way to their designated range.

Chapter 5

Stick and Rudder vs. the Microchip

It's an hour's ride on a diesel-powered Blue Goose Air Force bus to the Indian Springs Auxiliary Airfield some fifty miles northwest of Nellis, and you have to be on the road at "O dark thirty" to make it in time for the first range event of the day. While the Gunsmoke teams have been preparing for their flights, the people assigned to the ranges located adjacent to Indian Springs have been equally busy setting up the ranges for the first aircraft arrival. Today's events on Range 63 will include Profile II bombing and strafing runs by three teams, two flying F-16s and the third flying A-10s. These two aircraft couldn't be any farther apart in the approach their designers took when creating them. On paper it looks like no contest, but that's not exactly how the respective pilots see it. The Warthog (A-10) aviators aren't intimidated, as one pilot commented:

"The technical disadvantage really doesn't mean anything. Computers make the job easy on the range; the A-10s [pilot] have to make lots of calculations as they dive toward the ground. The A-10 is a flying gun, an updated A-1 [Skyraider]. It's not as good at dropping bombs as the F-16, but as far as pilot skills, 'Hog drivers are much better than F-16 drivers."

One of his teammates followed with: "Let 'em have all the systems they want—we'll do just as well."

There are two standard range configurations at Indian Springs—two-tower or three-tower. Range 63 is a two-tower setup, with a sighting tower and a main control tower, and is one of the primary conventional air-to-ground ranges at Nellis. In the cab of the main tower, the Range Control Officer (RCO) is in contact with Nellis and each flight as they check onto the range. He is a rated officer and has absolute control of all range activity, both on the ground and in the air. He approves the request from each team to enter the range and to expend ordnance, and he's also charged with checking each pass to ensure that the aircraft stay inside the established boundaries. Cross-ing a boundary line brings a foul call and results in an unscored pass, something no Gunsmoke team can afford.

As cold as it is on the Nellis flightline before dawn, temperatures are even lower at the range. Nothing stands between you and the wind blowing off the mountains to the west. Even as the sun comes up, revealing the expanse of sand, dirt and scrub brush that is the range, it will be hours before the temperature starts to rise. For that reason, an early range time provides some advantage for the teams that draw them; the air is cool and there are few thermals rising from the desert to rock and buffet the aircraft as they dive toward their targets. Every little bit helps.

Downrange, ground crews are setting up the strafe panels, giant white squares of cloth twenty-five feet on a side, marked with a four-foot bull's-eye in the center of each panel. Four of these "rags" hang from metal cables attached to telephone poles at the end of each strafing range. The crews take the panels out to their positions in the back of four-wheel-drive pickups. The off-road capability doesn't really seem necessary until you open the door and leap out, promptly sinking up to your shins in the fine white powder that covers the strafe range to a depth of a couple of feet. The dirt fills your shoes and a cloud of white dust is rising toward your face as your driver, one of the senior range NCOs, gives you a big grin and waves you on out to the target location. Even with no airplanes in the vicinity, it's discomforting to find yourself standing just below the bull's-eye of one of the target panels, listening with one ear to your guide's spiel while your head swivels constantly, searching for the single airplane that you know somehow has made it onto the range unnoticed.

The bombing target, located on the opposite side of the range complex, is an olive-drab tank, sitting in the middle of nothing but sand and stunted desert bushes. From the shadows below the range tower the tank is difficult to see with the naked eye, and only marginally easier through a telephoto lens. It's even tougher to pick

out from the cockpit of a moving aircraft several hundred feet above the desert floor.

While the range crews raise the rags into position on the strafe range, the Ford Aerospace contractor personnel who run the visual scoring system start the checks on their equipment. The Television Ordnance Scoring System (TOSS) is basically the computerized version of the manual system used on many ranges. In the manual version, observers at two different points plot each bomb impact using periscopes marked with aiming circles and crosshairs. The two plots are compared and the precise point of impact can be determined. Using TOSS, two television cameras on each of two range towers scan the bomb impact. The system operator places a cursor over the impact point and a computer calculates the actual distance from the target, based on the presurveyed location of the cameras.

Safety on the Nellis ranges is, in the words of a time-honored Air Force cliche, paramount. The Range Control Officer must monitor all the radio traffic on the range, and each team checks in with the RCO as they approach the range complex. After departing Nellis, the teams transit either Range 62 or 64 and then proceed to their assigned range, where they enter downwind at the altitude for the highest pattern they will fly. The first team is on the range and, as the lead turns final and drops his aircraft's nose toward the target, he calls in, "MACE 11, in hot."

"Roger, cleared," crackles over the radio from the RCO, and the pilot is into his first live pass.

All of the bombing patterns flown at Gunsmoke, whether level, low-angle or high-angle dive, require the solution of the same basic bombing triangle problem. To place a bomb on a given target, the impact point is calculated based upon three variables: air speed, altitude and range to the target. If each of those is known precisely by the pilot, the aircraft can be set up to display a release point that will ensure the bomb falls exactly in the center of the target, or a "shack" as they call it.

If it's that easy, why isn't every pass a shack? Basically because the winds, the airplane, the bomb and yes, even the pilot, don't always do what the calculations call for. The air speed portion of the equation must be exact; a few knots fast and the bomb will be long, a few knots slow and it will fall short of the target. The same results can come from the pilot hitting the "pickle button" a fraction

Two A-7Ds from the New Mexico ANG head for the range carrying BDU-33 25 lb. practice bombs mounted on their triple ejector racks. John Sheehan

of a second early or late. Calculations for a 20 degree dive pass will be thrown off if the airplane is actually diving at 19 or 21 degrees. And a bent fin on one of the BDU 33 practice bombs may upset its ballistics enough to screw up the most accurate set of calculations.

On today's Profile II passes, each aircraft will be executing what are called tactical patterns, distinguished from the routing box patterns used in Profile I by the requirement for the pilot to use terrain masking on the run toward the target, waiting until the last possible moment to gain altitude and set up for his bomb delivery. These "pop" patterns are realistic examples of the tactics any ground attack aircraft must employ to avoid enemy defenses surrounding an intended target. For safety reasons, the lower altitude limits for the bomb delivery portion of the pass are set fairly high:

- 1,000 ft. AGL (800 ft. for the A-10) for 20 degree low-angle low-drag (LALD)
- 200 ft. AGL for all aircraft for 10 degree low-angle high-drag (LAHD)
- 150 ft. AGL for all aircraft for 200 ft. AGL level bombing

Any pilot busting those lower altitude limits will get a foul call on the pass, resulting in a no score. The tactical patterns have some additional requirements that must be met to avoid penalties. An altitude window of between 100 ft. AGL and 300 ft. AGL must be observed on ingress to the target prior to the pop-up. Two judges with stopwatches and binoculars also monitor the pop-up passes for exposure time, or the time an aircraft would be exposed to enemy defenses. Exposure timing starts when the pilot initiates pull-up for the pop, and the judges see nose rota-

F-4Es from the 3rd TFW, Clark AFB, ready for the day's mission at Gunsmoke 1989. Ian Francis

tion. The timing stops when the bomb comes off of the aircraft. The judges are watching for a maximum of twenty-five seconds' exposure in the 10 degree low-angle high-drag dive, and 30 seconds for the 20 degree low-angle low-drag.

Although it takes five pages of text and eight separate charts to explain in the Gunsmoke Official Rules, the bombing events scoring system is relatively straightforward.

In Profile II, for the twenty degree LALD event, each bomb landing within three meters of the target is worth 125 points; bombs in excess of three meters cost three points for each additional meter.

Ten degree LAHD bombs within three meters of the target also receive 125 points; in excess of three meters, they cause a deduction of four points per meter.

In the 200 ft. AGL level bombing event, bombs placed within three meters of the target again are scored at 125 points; over three meters, each bomb costs two points per meter.

Assuming two perfect passes for each Profile II event, the maximum Profile II scores are 250 points per aircrew, 1,000 points per team, or 3,000 points for the three events.

Judges in the Range Control tower monitor each aircraft on its bombing run, watching for excess dive angles, violation of minimum altitude restrictions and excessive exposure time during the pop-up portion of the pass.

Markings on the windows of the RCO tower cab allow the judges to determine dive angles. Five degrees of excessive dive angle results in a foul, or no points for that pass. Minimum altitude violations are also scored at zero

This F-16 lifts off on a range mission with the Nellis tower in the background. Ian Francis

points, while excessive exposure time during pop-up is penalized five points per second over the maximum allowable time.

The level bombing passes must be made at 200 ft. AGL, with a 150 ft. AGL foul altitude. If the aircraft is above 300 ft. when the pop is initiated, no points are awarded for that pass. The level bomb event at past Gunsmoke meets would be a no score if any dive angle was seen during the pass. That restriction was removed for the 1989 competition, and a maximum dive angle of 3 degrees is allowed.

On base leg, each aircraft is flying at between 100 and 200 ft. AGL. They make their turn and pop-up to their weapons delivery altitude, climbing at around 5 degrees more than the dive angle that will be used (a 25 degree climb on a 20 degree low-angle pass). At the top of the climb, the pilot rolls into the target and sets up his dive angle. Coming down the chute, the A-10A will be diving at somewhere between 350 and 375 knots (kts), while the faster airplanes will be doing 375 to 400 kts. Hence the need for the lower 1,000 ft. foul altitude for the A-10.

A former A-10A driver expounded on the Warthog's air speed: "In most aircraft, the airspeed indicator doubles as a machmeter. In the A-10, it doubles as a calendar."

As the aircraft drops down the chute toward the target, the pilot works to hold air speed and dive angle steady, fighting the crosswinds and thermals that try to move his jet off of its ideal course. The A-10A and the

A Pave Tack laser pod mounted on the centerline station of a 3rd TFW F-4E. Gunsmoke 89 marked the first year the Pave Tack system was used in this competition. It provided increased bombing accuracy for the crews from Clark AFB, and helped them take home the trophy as the top F-4 team for that year. Ian Francis

F-4s are in their element here, both large, heavy aircraft that are hard to budge once they are set up and dropping toward the tank waiting below them.

The A-10A pilot continued: "The A-7 and the F-4 have been around for over 20 years but they're still valid weapons systems—that's why we have them. They come out here every time and do well—A-7s usually finish in the top three. The A-7 in essence is the progenitor of the F-16; the technology of the A-7 was refined for the F-16."

Here's where all that technology pays off for the F-16. Its fully automated bombing suite, controlled by the Stores Management System (SMS), takes information received from the fire control radar (target range), the radar altimeter (aircraft altitude), includes the air speed

and dive angle information available to the onboard computer, and calculates the precise release point for the type of weapon in use. The release point is displayed as a symbol on the HUD (head up display) for the pilot; when he flies the aircraft to direct the HUD symbol through the target, the SMS transmits a release signal to the appropriate wing pylon and the bomb is ejected from the triple ejector rack, or TER.

How accurate does that make the F-16? Maj. Gen. Billy G. McCoy, Tactical Fighter Weapons Center commander, explained: "The flying was superb. . . . "The best dive bomb sortie hit the tank turret with three out of four bombs. In the low angle high drag bomb category, three participants put 17 of their 24 bombs in the tank turret. In

Loaded and ready to roll, an F-4E of the 924th TFG, Bergstrom AFB, Texas, gets a final check from the ground crew prior to taxiing. Ian Francis

level bombing, the top six fliers hit the turret with 16 of their 24 bombs. . . ."

Where does all this smoke and mirrors technology leave the teams flying other aircraft? Compared to the F-16, one A-10 pilot said: "I liken it to me challenging you to multiply 50 numbers—you do it longhand and I'll use a calculator. There's no comparison. What counts is experience in the aircraft. We have to fly the aircraft and get the bomb to the target; they have to just let the aircraft take them to the target."

Another A-10 pilot said: "The A-10A is a lot harder to work; it's strictly manual, with no computers whatsoever. The F-16 had radar for ranging—it tells the computer that the bomb will get from here to there at this point, then the pilot pickles."

"We have to arrive at a certain point in the sky at the right airspeed, the right altitude, the right dive angle and the pipper has to be on the target. You have to guess what the winds are doing—if all five of these things come together at the same time, you hit the target," according to another pilot.

A fourth pilot added, "It's like throwing a rock out of your car window as you go by!"

Being away from home station makes a big difference on the bombing runs. Nellis is a real change from places farther east, such as Indiana or Connecticut—about 2,000

An A-10A two-ship element heads for the Nellis range complex as this F-16 in the foreground awaits its pilot. Ian Francis

feet higher and with fewer geographical references like trees.

One A-10 pilot stated: "The low altitude events—level bomb, low angle dive—are sight picture bombs. You have to think like a BDU; roll on in, say that looks about right—if I were a bomb I'm gonna hit, then you pickle. It's easy with trees to judge height. Nellis looks like the back side of the moon—you go, that looks about right, pow!, and the bomb drops two miles short."

Another pilot commented: "Density altitude is a real problem. We normally work with 1,000 to 1,500 ft. at home. Here it's 3,500 to 4,000 ft.—it makes a big difference. The airplane flies like it's at 4,000 ft. when we start out. On a 20 degree pop-up the F-16s will just come in, go to burner and they pull up. We have to start out in the ionosphere, drop on down and then pop."

"Gunsmoke is not geared to what the A-10 does in combat. You wouldn't drop Mk 82s from a 20 degree pop in an A-10 because it would stall before you got the nose down," said another A-10 driver.

All that being said, the judges in the Gunsmoke rules meeting make it clear to the participants that this is not a tactical event. They're not here to judge tactics, they're here to see how close each pilot can put bombs on the target or how many bullets he can put through the rag.

The F-4 crews have to work with virtually the same handicaps as the A-10As. Some of the Rhinos at Gunsmoke are over twenty-one years old and while they do have a dive/toss-bombing system, it was developed in the 1960s and it's strictly mechanical—no digital computers here. An ANG F-4 team leader discussed his team's experience with the system:

A front view of the tracking equipment on the Nellis bombing ranges. The operator uses the center sight to follow the aircraft as they make their passes, while the attached television cameras feed *pictures back to Nellis where live commentary is provided on each aircraft's performance.* Ian Fancis

TV cameras and microwave antennas mounted on the range tower at Nellis Range 63 near the Indian Springs Air Force Station, north of Nellis AFB. The cameras are part of the Television Ordnance Scoring System (TOSS) which gives computerized bomb scores for each of the Gunsmoke teams. John Sheehan

"Two of the crews used it on the first day and got 20 meter bombs—we're looking for one meter. That's as good as we can get out of the system. The other two [which struck much closer] were 450 knot manual bombs! We're the least technological aircraft out here."

There was a ray of hope for the F-4 troops, however. The 3rd TFW from Clark AB, Republic of the Philippines, flying F-4Es, came to town with some high-tech machinery grafted on to their Phantoms. For the first time in the history of Gunsmoke, the judges ruled that use of the PAVE TACK laser designator was permitted and the 3rd TFW, with a little over a year's experience on the system, was ready to put it to work. Carrying the same PAVE TACK equipment as the F-111Fs from the 48th TFW at RAF Lakenheath, England, used on their raid over Libya, these F-4Es are now capable of finding targets, designating them with an onboard laser and then releasing a laser-guided bomb (LGB), or "smart bomb," that will fly down the laser beam until impact. That's great, but no one's dropping LGBs at Gunsmoke, so where does PAVE TACK fit in? One of the 3rd TFW crews explained it this way: "PAVE TACK can be used for dropping 'dumb' bombs—the laser provides ranging information to the ARN-101 weapons system and navigation computer and this gives us the target elevation," said one crew member.

The WSO commented: "We roll on in, fire the laser at the target. It's married up to the sight; when he [the pilot] hits the pickle button it instantly reads out the altitude at that time. It's pure ranging. It cleans out all the other anomalies in the system. It's the most accurate information you can get—real hard target altitude."

"It still requires a manual release. We boresight the ARN-101 computer with the gunsight in the attack mode. We sight on a water tower at the end of the runway, then we set the PAVE TACK pod on the same target. When we come down the chute, the continuously computed impact point (CCIP) rolls across the ground in the sight as we go, so when I pickle, the cross hairs on the PAVE TACK pod should be on the same spot—that stabilizes the sight picture from the pod on the pickle point. He [the WSO] can see the impact point and we can score the bomb from the cockpit—say 15 ft. at 12 o'clock—and we can correct for it on the next pass," said the pilot.

Crews from the 3rd TFW had peaked up the systems and their jets at Clark AB in the Philippines, and were dropping less than ten-meter bombs, with the average at eight meters. Their goal was to be able to drop seven-meter bombs if they were to be competitive. The PAVE TACK system gave them those extra few meters.

The bombing events highlight the contrast in the aircraft's capabilities like nothing else. Early on, it's apparent that an F-16 team will take home the bombing honors and

An A-10A banks hard left as the pilot pulls away from the target tank, seen to the right of the smoke burst. Ian Francis

the other competitors will have to fight for the runner-up positions. Pass after pass, the pilots in F–16s are dead on the target, a "shack," while other aircraft must be satisfied with bombs landing several meters away from the tank. An F–4 crew will take a three-meter bomb any day, while the F–16 pilots are having a bad day if they don't hit the tank on most of their passes. After the bombs are scored and the tapes are reviewed, it's clear that the F–16s are not just hitting the tank, they're bouncing BDU–33s off the tank turret on pass after pass. Pilot skill plays a part in any

of the Gunsmoke events, but in the bombing profiles the computerized bomb delivery system on the F–16 is hard to beat. *Impossible* to beat, as it turns out, for the F–4, A–7 and A–10 teams.

F–16 teams took the top spots in all of the bombing events but there was some consolation for the 3rd TFW team—one of their crews placed fifth in the 30 degree dive-bomb competition, which put them ahead of several F–16 outfits for that one event. Quite a performance for the aging Phantoms from the Philippines.

A close-up view of a fully loaded TER, complete with three BDU–33 practice bombs. This shot clearly shows the streamers attached to the bomb rack safety pins, as well as the additional *streamers on safety blocks at the nose of each BDU–33.* Ian Francis

Chapter 6

Shootout

Once the bomb runs are complete, the team reverses its direction of flight and shifts over to the strafing range to take on the rags hanging at the far end. The strafe event is one of the great levelers; pilot skill really determines the score here, and no single aircraft type has an advantage. The F-16 is certainly able to strafe as well as any other type, but loses the clear advantage it enjoys in the bombing events.

Low-angle strafing passes are flown at between 5 and 15 degrees of dive angle, with each team's aircraft allowed a maximum of three runs down the range. Strafe scores are based on the number of holes in each aircraft's rag, less the number of rounds fired in excess of the authorized 100 rounds. For example, a pilot who fired 108 rounds and hit the rag 75 times would be assessed a score of 67.

Due to the differences in each aircraft's gun system, more than 100 rounds of ammunition are allowed to be loaded. The munitions judges verify the actual number of rounds delivered and loaded in each aircraft.

As an example, a small number of dummy rounds of 20 mm ammunition is necessary in the M61A1 gun system to ensure the entire ammunition path is filled, allowing the gun to operate.

Some aircraft types are equipped with a cockpit rounds counter which tells the pilot the number of rounds fired. In the other aircraft, the pilot must estimate and stop firing when he thinks he has fired 100 rounds.

In both Profile I and II, the strafing runs are made at between five and fifteen degrees for all aircraft, with a minimum altitude restriction of seventy five ft. AGL. A foul line is established at 2,000 ft. in front of the strafe targets.

Each pilot can score a maximum of 250 points in the strafe events, or 2.5 points per bullet. In addition to the points subtracted for every hit over 100, the pilots are looking at a fifty-percent reduction in their score for a run if they press past the 2,000 ft. foul line in front of the

Squadron patch of one of the crew members assigned to 3rd TFW, Clark AB, Republic of the Philippines. John Sheehan

targets, fire double bursts, are guilty of a lazy pull-off at the end of a pass, use less than a 5 degree dive angle or drop below 75 ft. AGL. An experienced pilot on a good strafe pass will wait until the last second to squeeze the trigger, cutting the distance to the rags, and he'll complete the burst at just a hair in front of the 2,000 ft. foul line.

After all passes are complete, range personnel pull down the rags, heave them into the back of a pickup truck and drive them back to the range control tower area. The targets are laid out on the ground and judges pore over each one, a can of spray paint in hand to mark every hole left by the projectiles. The goal—a hundred rounds fired and a hundred holes in the rag; not easy to achieve, but not impossible. It's been done, not once but twice, and by a Warthog driver at that. Great shooting in anybody's book. The pilot who fired those perfect scores summed it up this way: "The F-16 gun is much smaller, with much more dispersion of the rounds. It's very hard to maintain so it consistently shoots [a pattern like] a small funnel. The A-10 holds a real tight dispersion . . . the hard part is when we pull the trigger. The gun tends to bounce around so much, it tends to travel. That's where the pilot comes in—putting it there, holding it there for the 0.3 to 0.6 seconds for the burst. We may have to put control inputs in to drive it back onto the target."

He continued: "On my gun I know exactly where it's going to go for 30 rounds, 40 rounds, 50 round bursts—it's different each time, so I sway the stick in the proper direction. . . . The gun, I feel, is man versus man."

The Phantoms with their internal guns have slightly more dispersion to contend with than the much newer F-16s. Even with the more experienced aircrews, the F-4 drivers were looking at scores in the high 70s or low 80s, while the F-16s and A-10s are routinely in the upper 90s. In a change from previous Gunsmoke practice, the strafe events are now broken up and flown on separate profiles. The final scores are not released until the end of the meet.

The difference in aircraft gun systems is dramatic from the vantage point of an observer on the range. The three different jets firing their 20 mm M61A1 internal cannon roll onto the final leg of their strafe passes and are virtually silent as they approach the targets. A twisting stream of white smoke flowing back from the front of the

Close-up view of only a small percentage of the A-10A's General Electric GAU-8 Avenger 30 mm cannon. The remainder of the tank-killing gun takes up the lower portion of the fuselage from the leading edge of the wing forward to the nose of the aircraft. When the gun is removed for maintenance, a tail jack is needed to keep the Warthog from sitting smartly on its butt. John Sheehan

Range crews pull down the first of four 25 x 25 ft. rags used as strafe targets on the Nellis ranges. After each team has made their strafing passes, the rags will be taken back to the range tower for scoring by operations judges. Ian Francis

fuselage is the first indicator that the pilot has fired, followed closely by the sound of the gun, a muted noise like a small piece of cloth being torn.

When the Warthogs roll in, their green and gray European I camouflage stands out against the blue sky and the muted earthtones of the desert. Much larger than their competitors, they seem to float in toward the targets with no detectable noise from their two T34 turbofan engines preceding them. The silence of their approach is shattered when the pilot triggers his GAU-8A 30 mm cannon. The nose of the aircraft disappears in a cloud of gun gas exhaust, and the sound of each projectile leaving the muzzle at over 3,500 ft. per second is like a chain saw ripping through solid oak.

For this Gunsmoke, the perfect 200 score fired by an A-10 jock summed up the strafe event. When all the bullets were counted, Warthog drivers were sitting in the top three spots, trailed by F-16 pilots holding down fourth and fifth place.

Strafe passes completed, the team members safe up their armament system switches, clear the range with the RCO and depart for the return to Nellis. Each team makes

next page
An A-10A pulls sharply off of a strafing run on the Nellis range. The Euro I camouflage keeps down the reflections even in the intense Nevada sun, but a glint from the canopy and the clearly visible white markings above the nose-mounted inflight refueling receptacle door make the aircraft easy to track in these conditions. The widely separated engine pods are designed to keep damage or fire in one engine from spreading to the other. The horizontal stabilizer also provides some masking from the ground for the exhaust of the two turbofan engines, a help in reducing the threat from heat-seeking missiles. John Sheehan

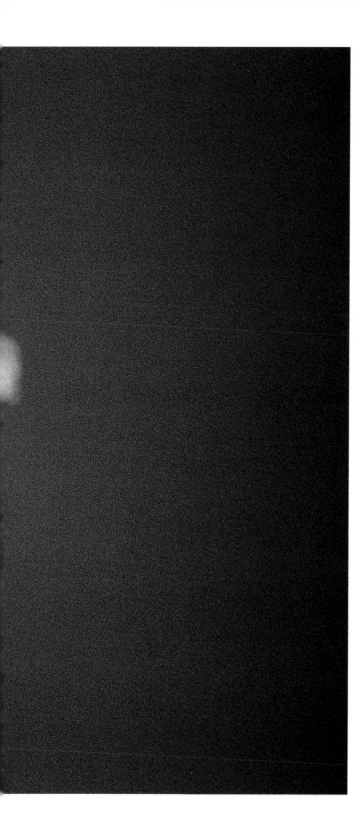

a high pass over the airfield and one by one the individual aircraft execute a tactical break out of the formation and into the landing pattern. They arrive with a crowd of well-wishers on hand, pull into the chocks and shut down. As the pilots move down the ladders to the ground, it's evident from the looks on their faces who had a good ride and who didn't.

The crews head back to their offices in the Red Flag building for another critique and some soul searching if needed. What went wrong, who did good and what can we do the next time to keep the scores up are the topics for discussion. There's no room to let up with the constant pressure being put on by other teams. The overall lead in a Gunsmoke meet will change hands daily as new events are flown and the teams move into the thick of the competition. It's unlikely that a team could move from the back of the pack to take the lead, but the final position of the first four or five teams is in doubt until the last score is in.

The Warthog at work. The A-10A is a stable strafing platform and the GAU-8/A 30 mm cannon is extremely accurate—two qualities that help the 'Hog excel on the range and against its intended foe, Warsaw pact tanks. For a short time in the mid 1980s the A-10 fleet was fitted with gun gas diffusers mounted on the front of the GAU-8's barrels. The diffuser was designed to direct the cloud of gun gas under the fuselage to reduce problems caused when the gas is ingested by the A-10A's engines. While it looked good on paper, the diffuser was not particularly well balanced, causing vibrations during gun firing that eventually led to problems with the gun mounts in the fuselage. John Sheehan

The 3rd TFW load crew removes 20 mm shell casings from one of their F-16s after a range mission. Ammunition is counted before and after each strafe mission to determine exactly how many rounds were fired; this number is then matched against the hits on the pilot's strafe target. John Sheehan

Gunsmoke judges at the range going over one of the strafe targets, or rags, and marking the hits with spray paint. The 25x25 ft. targets, with a 4 ft. bull's-eye, look fairly large in this view, but they don't seem to be quite the same size to a pilot coming down the chute on a strafing run. John Sheehan

Chapter 7

Low Level to Tolicha

Following the box pattern and tactical pattern profiles are the navigation-attack missions, Profile III. Each team member is tasked to fly two different low-level routes as part of a two-ship flight, once in the lead position and once as wingman. The profile rules call for each aircraft to put two inert Mk 82 500 lb. bombs, configured with BSU 49

"Hook 'em horns!" A 924th pilot flashes the traditional University of Texas sign as he guides his Phantom out of the chocks. Ian Francis

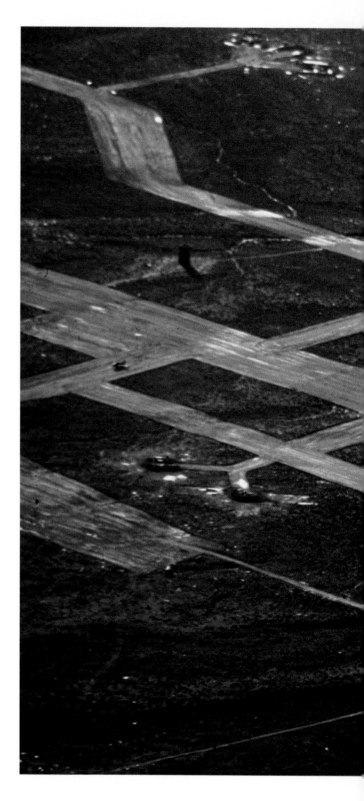

Air Inflated Retarder fin sets, onto the target, using time between the two aircraft to provide separation from simulated bomb fragment damage.

Nav-attack is basically a two-part scenario, requiring accurate navigation to the target and then a successful attack by the two aircraft using tactical delivery methods (the pop-up techniques also flown on Profile II). The target area for this event is the Tolicha airfield complex, an "enemy" airfield located on Nellis Range 76 up toward Tonapah, Nevada, in the Sun Valley-Mt. Helen area. The Gunsmoke crews are looking for a single aircraft out of some eighty total hidden in simulated aircraft revetments on the field. Set up primarily for the Red Flag exercises, targets on this range complex are meant to represent the bad guys' rear area, normally requiring the services of specialized long-range interdiction aircraft such as the F-111 or the F-15E Strike Eagle. (Remember the A-10 pilot's comments about not dropping Mk 82s from a pop pattern in the 'Hog.)

This is Gunsmoke, however, not Red Flag, and Tolicha is close enough for government work. Profile III is designed to test the teams' navigation skills combined with an attack "fragged" (from fragmentary orders) with a specific time-on-target (TOT). It's a pretty realistic scenario with application to actual combat conditions, so there's not much behind-the-scenes griping to be heard. Each aircraft is configured with the two 500 lb. bombs, as well as onboard infrared countermeasure flares, used to decoy enemy heat-seeking missiles. At 10 A.M. the day prior to the mission, the pilots get their route maps, which show nothing more than the circled turn points and the arrival time at each point. It's up to the crews to come up with the precise location of each point, as well as the headings required to each one. The 200 mile routes contain five scored turn points: the entry point, two enroute turn points, the initial point and the exit point. The F-4s, A-7s and F-16s fly the routes at 480—500 kgs (knots ground speed), while the A-10s are allowed to fly at 270 kgs. The only problem with the Warthogs using 480 knots is that

A portion of the simulated airfield that serves as the target for the nav-attack missions. Target aircraft are in the revetment in the upper portion of the picture. TSgt. Jose Lopez, Jr., AAVS

An A-10A jinks through simulated SAM and AAA (anti aircraft artillery) fire as the pilot sets up the aircraft for his run on the target. TSgt. Jose Lopez, Jr., AAVS

they would have to fly thirty knots faster than their maximum design air speed. (A well-worn Air Force joke says that the A-10 is the only aircraft in the inventory where the rear of the canopy has to be bird-resistant.)

The five scored turn points, which include the exit point, are marked by two 10x20 ft. cloth panels separated by 200 meters. These panels are aligned perpendicular to the course run-in and serve as "gates." One aircraft from the flight must pass between the panels within five seconds of the scheduled time. Passing through a gate plus or minus five seconds from the calculated time is worth 100 points. For each five seconds additional time, the team member is docked twenty points. Each aircrew can achieve a total of 900 points for a nav-attack mission, or a total of 1,800 points for the two missions flown in Profile III.

Although the crews can navigate to within a mile or so of each turn point, they have to get a visual on the panels and may have to put some Gs on the aircraft to get it on course before they pass the gate. The aircrews make a radio call in the blind—not to any specific receiver, no reply expected—when passing each checkpoint; in addition, they must call in as they hit the initial point and again when they are thirty seconds out from the target. The flights are required to be in a tactical formation which has the wingman trailing the lead aircraft by 3,000 to 9,000 feet at a 30 to 60 degree angle. Any other formation loses the team 250 points.

Each two-ship element flies the low-level portion of the profile between 100 and 500 feet AGL, although brief excursions to 700 feet are permitted "in the interest of flight safety" (such as avoiding large, immovable rock formations) and for tactically sound maneuvering. One aircraft in the flight must fly through each gate and flights are not allowed to cut off route segments to make up time. The aircraft must stay subsonic at all times on Profile III. Timing is handled by two rated officers who serve as timing judges at each gate. Both judges have digital watches hacked against the Range Control Center atomic clock prior to departure in the morning and again after arrival at Nellis that same evening. Times shown by the more accurate watch are used.

Flight leads develop target tactics which provide for individual level or low-angle high-drag deliveries on the same target, with minimum exposure. A thirty-second

A Gunsmoke judge positioned in the luxuriant foliage of the Nevada desert watches an A-10A depart the nav-attack course. Couldn't someone have at least found a chair for this guy? SSgt. David Nolan, AAVS

clearance time between aircraft at the target is imposed to simulate the spacing required to protect the wingman from the lead aircraft's bomb fragments. This frag clearance requirement is taken seriously—the second aircraft to drop receives a score of zero if his bombs impact less than twenty-six seconds after the first aircraft's bomb impact. Any aircrew dropping a bomb outside of seventy-six meters from the target also gets a goose egg (zero) for the event, and rightly so.

As part of the simulated combat scenario, surface-to-air missile (SAM) attacks are provided courtesy of Smokey SAM rockets launched from the range area. These overgrown versions of model rockets leave a thick smoke trail as they head, unguided, for the sky to provide some realism

during the attack missions. Another part of that same realism is the requirement for the attacking aircraft to expend flares during the pop-up. Flares will not be fired for more than ten seconds, and must be used only during the phase of the attack between pull-up and pull-down. In the event a level delivery is used, flares are expended beginning a maximum of one mile prior to bomb release. The maximum pop-up exposure time for nav-attack is thirty seconds, judged in the same way as the pop patterns in Profile II. After bomb release, each aircrew descends to 500 feet AGL or below for the leg to the egress gate.

Points are awarded as follows: The five turn points are each worth 100 points, use of infra-red flares is worth fifty points, a total of 400 points is possible for hitting the

Team members from the 181st TFG, Hullman Field, Indiana, hit the books as they go over plans for the next day's events. Ian Francis

target (250 points for the bomb and 150 points for time-on-target) and a further fifty points are awarded at the egress point. Five points are deducted for every second of excess exposure.

One would expect Profile III to be another event where the F-16s have the advantage, using their computerized navigation system to get them through the gates and in to the target with split-second accuracy. The other Gunsmoke teams acknowledge the worth of the F-16's avionics, but they don't see the nav-attack event as completely one-sided.

"Low-level nav-attack is the A-10's forte; we fly lots of low level navigation training missions," said one team member.

Another Gunsmoke competitor commented: "It's more difficult in the A-10 than the A-7 or F-16. For the F-16s, if they want to be at the start point at 11:30, they set that time into the system, tell it what time it is now, and then they get a little caret [symbol] on the HUD that says go faster."

"The A-10s are out there saying, well, about four seconds early, lets pull it back a little, that's about right.

A Gunsmoke team relaxes during a lull in the competition. The boards at the rear of the room hold a map of the Nellis ranges and a chalkboard to keep track of the team's progress in each event. Ian Francis

The INS will tell you how far it is to the target, but with only 0.8 of a mile accuracy—that's about plus or minus 12 seconds," added another pilot.

In the words of another competitor: "The fast movers can go over a mountain in burner and maintain ground-speed—in an A-10 you have to go around the mountain and lose a minute or so, then we don't know how late we are. It's strictly old Lindbergh across the ocean stuff—really antiquated."

"One advantage is that the ground goes by a lot slower in the A-10. That gives us time to read the maps and tell pretty close where we are," another team member said.

Another Gunsmoke participant stated: "[Nav-attack] is back to the basic pilot skills of piloting and navigation. A-10 pilots are much better [at those] than F-16 pilots. We're more than willing to turn off our INS and have the F-16s do the same thing and go out and fly."

"The F-16 has a great system but they're going to have to go to a manual tracking method somehow to check the computer. The caret will get them there plus or minus a few seconds, but just like the arrival competition there were some A-10s in the top five. There's a bit of luck involved. Their system is based on radar, they're dealing with winds a second to a second and a half old. What happens with wind shear or temperature inversions?

We've got two pilots who've put the airplane on time three times in a row—we don't know how they do it, and they don't know how they do it!" according to another pilot.

One F-16 team leader summed up the importance of the nav-attack profile: "Nav-attack will separate the winners. It's easier to lose Gunsmoke flying nav-attack. The other events are the preliminary to what makes Gunsmoke what it is. In nav-attack, you control your own destiny. . . . We had a bad INS on one airplane; rather than change the INS and add an unknown quantity, we used the spare aircraft, which was a known quantity."

It is possible to game the nav-attack missions, though. By flying the wing, a pilot gains a little extra time to check out the area, find the target and complete his attack, hopefully scoring some extra points. If he takes the lead on the first flight, and is lucky enough to score well, he's got the advantage of flying wing on the second flight and using the extra time available to get those additional points.

As one of the A-10 drivers put it, "Flying the A-10 takes more experience than magic." Even so, the latest Profile III winner at Gunsmoke was flying an F-16 and scored 1,796 points out of a possible 1,800. The number two through four slots were occupied by other F-16 pilots. A Warthog jock made it into the number five position with 1,706 points on the scoreboard. Maybe a little magic isn't so bad after all.

Chapter 8

Hanging Iron

Spread out among the flying events are the aircraft weapons loading contests, or the Loadeo competition. Each team's load crew must compete in two separate events, a static load where six inert Mk 82 bombs are loaded on a team aircraft against the clock, and an integrated combat turnaround, the ICT, designed to simulate the servicing and reloading of an aircraft returning from a combat sortie.

The static load is worth a maximum of 1,500 points, as is the ICT. However, the two loads are not tracked separately. A single munitions score is determined by adding the static load and ICT points, with a maximum possible of 3,000 points. The winning munitions score in 1989 was 2,910 points.

Both events are similar in that they revolve around loading bombs on the aircraft, but past that point they are drastically different. The static load involves only the load crew, while the ICT takes the load crew, aircraft crew chiefs and refueling specialists to complete. In many cases, Gunsmoke teams also use their pilots (and WSOs) as part of the ICT crew to provide an extra pair of hands and to demonstate that the aircrew is an integral part of the operation. A little showmanship is always appropriate at Gunsmoke.

Providing a good example of the multitude of skills required to get a combat aircraft back in the air ready to fight again, the ICTs at Gunsmoke are intense events that really put the pressure on a team's ground crews. Because the flying events are scheduled during the morning, the ICTs must start at noon or later. By then, the ramp at Nellis is baking, with heat pouring up from the concrete. There is no shade other than what little can be found under an aircraft wing or in the shadow of a truck. No hats are permitted on the flightline, so the folks with little or no hair on top are in trouble, sporting scalps the color of well-cooked lobsters by the second or third day of the meet.

Each Loadeo event is run against the clock, with the optimum times for each event broken down according to aircraft type; as shown in this chart:

Aircraft type	ICT	Static load
A–7	25 min.	37 min.
A–10	23 min.	30 min.
F–4	24 min.	35 min.
F–16	18 min.	34 min.

These times are adjusted for each competition and are based on the average times of previous Gunsmoke loading events. As each team strives to achieve a lower load time, the time requirements drop. In past meets, ½ point was awarded to a load crew for each minute they were below the optimum loading time. The judges eventually came to see this practice as having a negative impact, encouraging crews to hurry at the expense of safety, and it has been discontinued.

The ICTs are events that bring into focus the artificialities present in any competition. Although a combat turn could be conducted on an open ramp in wartime, a more realistic location would be in one of the several types of hardened aircraft shelters (HAS) found on overseas airbases. Throw in the requirement to wear a full chemical warfare ensemble and to operate inside a closed HAS with several pieces of diesel-powered support equipment in operation and you've got a scene straight out of a load crew's worst nightmare. Not to worry, during Gunsmoke it's all done in the open on the ramp with everyone dressed in summer-weight uniforms.

The team's ICT crew assembles at their designated spot on the ramp, where the turn area, 100 feet on a side, has been marked off by ropes and stanchions. Two areas are normally set up, with two sets of bleachers back to back for the spectators.

The necessary ground support equipment, or AGE (aerospace ground equipment), is on hand. This includes the MHU 110 trailer carrying the six inert Mk 82 bombs and their inert M 904 fuses; an MJ-1 bomb lift truck, known on the flightline as a "jammer"; and an A/M32A-60 generator set used to provide aircraft electrical power and compressed air for engine starts. The R-9 refueling truck is nearby, and a Halon 1211 flightline fire extinguisher is positioned near the aircraft. The load crew has on hand its tool box and assorted items of personal equipment used during the load.

A group of weapons judges is assigned to each loading event. All senior NCOs, the judges have extensive backgrounds as "load toads" and supervisors; they will watch every step of the ICT, looking for any violation of the technical order procedures involved or for any mistake that could impair the safety of the operation. The load crews that make it to Gunsmoke are good, and they don't make many mistakes. The judges don't miss the few that are made.

A typical ICT scenario calls for the turn director to position the aircraft in the chocks and establish interphone communication with the pilot. The ground crew checks the tires for cuts and uses a special wax pencil to do a hot brake check. Landing gear safety pins are installed if required, and the aircraft is chocked and grounded. On an F-16, the Emergency Power Unit safety pin is installed at this point. The turn supervisor checks in with the pilot and asks for his ammunition, fuel and liquid oxygen (LOX) requirements. The turn supervisor also has the pilot set up the appropriate cockpit switches for ground refueling, and ensures that the armament switches are safed. Now the pilot can shut down the engine and leave the cockpit.

The ground crew looks for any fluid leaks and ensures that any launchers, racks or pylons being carried are serviceable. The load crew preps the gun system for loading and does the same for the TER-9 on each wing. The mobile Ammunition Loading System (ALS) is positioned next to the aircraft gun and the feed head is connected to the internal gun. Ammunition is cranked into the gun system, the ALS is disconnected and removed and the gun system is closed up. Oil servicing is done as needed, and on an F-16 the LOX bottle and the onboard Halon explosion suppression system bottle are replaced if required.

The refueling truck moves into place and the fuel hose is unreeled and dragged over to the single point refueling receptacle (SPR) on the fuselage (the SPR for the A-10A is located in the front of the port landing gear pod). The refueling truck is grounded and then bonded to the aircraft, the fuel nozzle is connected, fuel flow starts and the ground

The business end of an inert Mk 82 500 lb. practice bomb. An M 904 fuse has been installed in the nose fusewell, and arming wire inserted through the hole in the fuse impeller. The arming wire is held in place by a Fahnstock clip to prevent the wire from being pulled out early. The other end of the wire is clipped into the MAU 12 bomb rack and stays with the aircraft once the bomb is released. The weight of the bomb overcomes the resistance of the clip and the wire is pulled out of the impeller, allowing it to turn freely in the airstream. After a certain number of turns to provide for the safe separation of the aircraft, the fuse arms and will detonate upon impact. John Sheehan

crew checks for airflow out of the fuel vents. Fueling an aircraft at nearly 50 psi of pressure with blocked fuel vents can possibly result in major damage to the fuel tanks with the risk of a resultant fire. With fueling complete, the fuel hose is removed and stowed on the R-9, and the grounding and bonding cables are disconnected.

Flare modules are loaded in the AN/ALE-40 dispensers on the aircraft and the required safety pins are inserted. All that remains is to install ejector carts in the wing pylons and TERs, load the bombs, install the various safety pins and tighten down the sway braces on each bomb and position the bomb rack ejector feet.

At the designated start time for the ICT, one of the team's aircraft taxis up to the parking spot and is marshaled into the chocks by the crew chief. The clock is running on the turnaround, and each of the team members moves with deliberate speed, trying to hurry and knowing that breaking into a run will drop points from the overall score. A crowd of onlookers has gathered in the bleachers, most to cheer on the home team, but a few from the opposition are also on hand to compare performances. As the load progresses, sweat begins to pour off of each team member. The pilot or crew is out of the cockpit and awaiting their opportunity to help out; the crew chief makes quick checks of aircraft systems while the load crew is working on their preload tasks. To an observer, the ICT is an unorganized mass of machinery and people that seems to avoid dissolving into chaos through sheer luck. In fact, each member of the team has practiced this scenario many times while preparing for Gunsmoke; everybody has a job and knows when and how to do it. The key to success in the ICT is no mistakes and a low overall time—faster than competing teams who have practiced equally hard and are certainly as determined to win this portion of Gunsmoke.

One crew member climbs into the cockpit, the -60 power cart is started and whines to life. With power on the aircraft the load crew can complete its preload tasks and get down to the serious business of loading. A second crew member works over the munitions trailer, preparing the inert Mk 82s for loading. Scrutinized by a judge, he has the unenviable task of preparing each of the six bombs, installing the M-904 fuse in the nose, running several pieces of steel arming wire down the bomb body to control fuse and retarder functions, and to keep out of the way of the other crew members as they load successive bombs.

The unofficial Gunsmoke motto, stenciled on an ammo can used to carry additional components on this munitions trailer. The load crew member is stringing arming wire on each bomb prior to its removal from the trailer. John Sheehan

The feed head of a 20 mm Ammunition Loading System is mated to the A–7D's gun system prior to cranking in ammunition as part of the ICT. Ian Francis

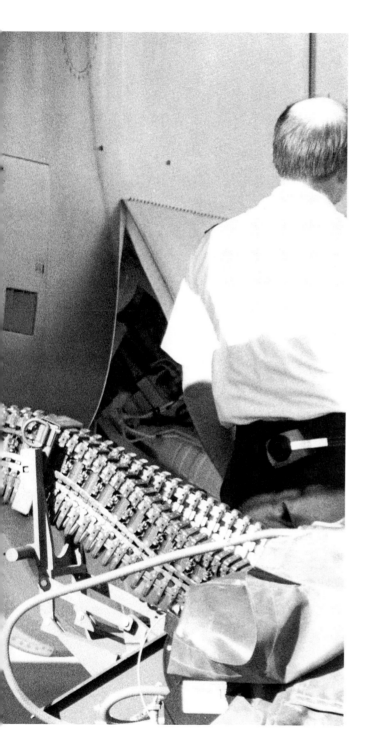

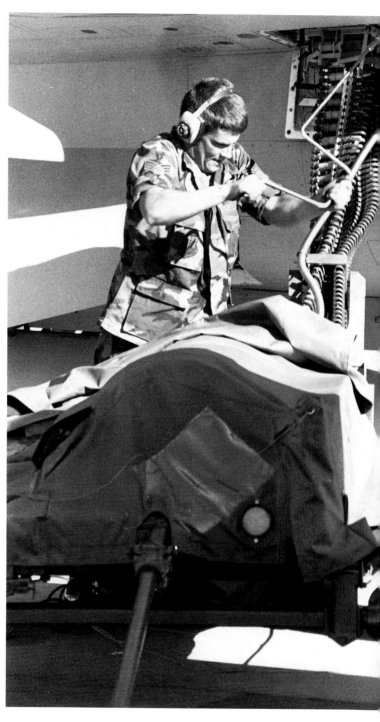

Not everything is power assisted as this loader finds out. He's using a speed handle to crank 20 mm shells from the ALS into the F-16's gun system. Ian Francis

The aircrews lend a hand here, rolling bombs forward on their chocks and passing tools or equipment to the loader working the bombs. As soon as a bomb is prepped, the load team chief moves in with the second team member who drives the MJ-1 jammer. This vehicle allows the crew to pick up the bomb on a hydraulic arm, move it to the aircraft and load it onto the chosen station with speed and precision.

While the jammer driver can make large corrections in the bomb position by using the steering wheel to turn the entire vehicle, the load crew chief takes care of the final critical adjustments with the hydraulic controls on the table at the end of the lift arm. These controls move the table, and the bomb on it, to the front or rear, side to side, and allow it to tilt as well. These minor adjustments are crucial in putting the two bomb lugs directly in line with the matching hooks at each station on the TER (triple ejector rack) loaded on each wing. A practiced crew can line up on the first try, but it's the exception rather than the rule. Once the team chief is happy with the bomb position, he signals the jammer driver who raises the lift arm to drive the bomb lugs into the rack—an operation that may lift the wing on an aircraft the size of an F-16. That's why they're called jammers. A turn of a wrench locks the bomb

A 432nd TFW "load toad" strings arming wire on inert Mk 82 500 lb. bombs during the team's ICT. Ian Francis

rack, the driver lowers the lift arm slightly and the bomb gets a "shake test" from the crew chief to verify that it's going to stay with the aircraft.

On the other side of the plane the refueling truck has fired up, moved to the side of the aircraft and the hose is reeled out and moved to the aircraft where the quick disconnect nozzle is locked into the universal refueling fitting. Refueling an aircraft with power on and bomb loading under way is inherently hazardous; each truck has been fitted with a "dead man" switch that controls the flow of fuel to the aircraft. This switch is held by a team member devoted to observing the activity around the jet and who will release the switch at the first sign of difficulty, instantly stopping fuel flow. Refueling must keep pace with the bomb loading—once the three bombs are loaded

on the opposite side, the load crew must move on to the second TER or lose time accordingly. The instant fueling stops, the hose is retracted onto its reel and the truck moves off, giving the load crew a clear shot at the second TER. Time is in short supply now and the final three bombs can win or lose the ICT event. The crew is into its well-practiced rhythm by this point and only an unforeseen glitch could shake their confidence. The crowd of supporters is keeping time and urging the crew on. Judges seem to be everywhere, able to mix with the action and yet avoid becoming obstacles or being run down by the moving equipment.

As the last bomb slams home into the rack, the crew chief gives it a shake, the jammer driver reverses sharply and parks and the whole crew moves over the aircraft,

With the ICT clock started, this load crew repositions inert Mk 82 bombs on the munitions trailer. These bombs still require arming *wire and nose fuses before they can be uploaded on the TER, hanging on the F-16 in the background.* Ian Francis

An ICT load crew member configures M 904 nose fuses during one of the Loadeo events at Nellis AFB. The inert Mk 82 500 lb. bombs are waiting on the munitions trailer, and a Halon flightline fire extinguisher is positioned in the background. Ian Francis

finishing up their postload tasks. The aircrew has tidied up the trailer, removing any debris and folding the bomb tie-down straps in neat piles. While the judges watch and wait, the final steps of the ICT are completed, the load crew assembles at the side of the aircraft and snap to attention at the crew chief's command. The ICT is over, stopwatches click and the crowd of onlookers signal their support with a variety of whistles, clapping and stomping feet.

While the load crew and the rest of the team await the final decision, the judges go over the aircraft one last time, checking the bombs on each station, looking at the condition of the tools and searching for any fault or error. They give the load crew a final briefing on their performance and their time, shake hands with each crew member and then fade away as the rest of the teams, family members and friends move past the ropes to congratulate the team.

*The pilot lends a hand during an ICT, sliding another inert Mk 82
out on to the extender rails which have been mounted on the MHU
110 munitions trailer.* Ian Francis

The load crew chief swings the jammer table around 90 degrees as he prepares to pick up another bomb from the munitions trailer. The smoke in the background is diesel exhaust from the R-9 refueler. Ian Francis

The load crew chief guides the jammer driver as he positions the lift arm and rollers to pick up a Mk 82 from its extension rails. Ian Francis

The load crew chief signals his jammer driver to stop as they position the table for lifting this Mk 82 bomb while a judge observes.
Ian Francis

*The load crew chief works with his jammer driver to position the
first Mk 82 for loading on the TER, while another loading judge
observes.* Ian Francis

This jammer driver is intent on his task as he uses both hands to position the table under a bomb. Ear defenders are required in the high-noise environment of an ICT. Ian Francis

This F-16 load crew gives a Mk 82 the shake test prior to backing the jammer out from under it. Better to find out it isn't locked in now than after the pilot starts rolling down the runway. Ian Francis

*The ICT is well under way as the first Mk 82 500 lb. bomb is loaded
on the inboard shoulder station of the TER of an F-16 from the
347th TFW, Moody AFB, Georgia.* Ian Francis

An F-16 ICT load crew hangs their second inert Mk 82 500 lb. bomb on a TER during a Gunsmoke Loadeo event. The bombs were configured with arming wire and fuses by another team member while they were on the munitions trailer. Ian Francis

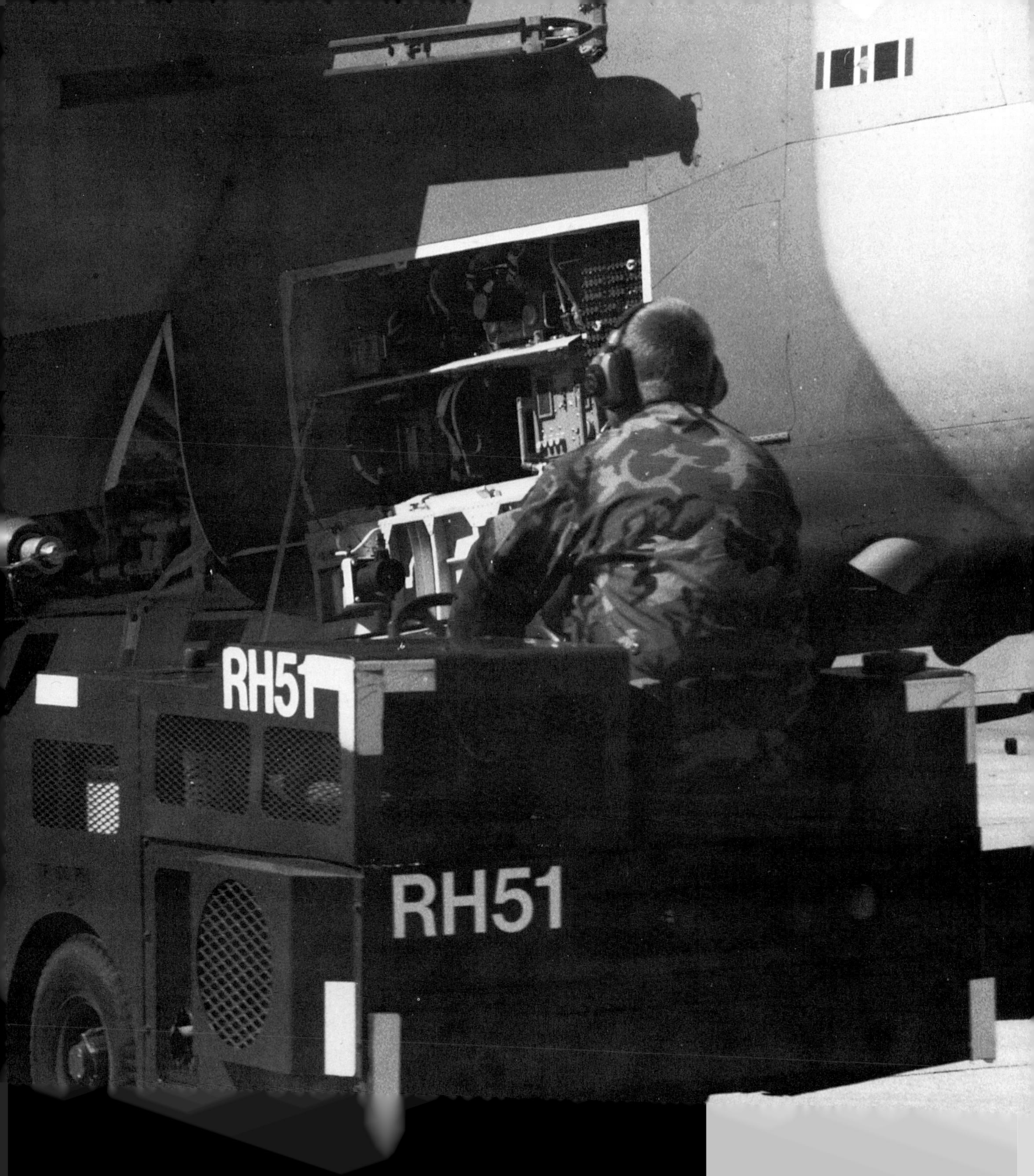
RH51
RH51

previous page
An A-7D load crew in ICT competition during the heat of the day
on the Nellis AFB ramp. The crew has its third Mk 82 ready to
upload on the centerline station of the TER. John Sheehan

The third Mk 82 goes up on the centerline TER station as the judges
look on. The fuel hose has filled out as fuel is transferred into an
F-16 from Moody AFB. Ian Francis

A load crew member makes some last minute adjustments during this F-16 ICT. Ian Francis

There's more than flying involved for a lot of the Gunsmoke air-crews. An integral part of the ICT team, this pilot squares away the munitions trailer after all the bombs have been loaded onto his F–16. Ian Francis

This ICT is down to the last few seconds. The pilot is checking the load of Mk 82 500 lb. bombs prior to his accepting the aircraft, as one of the load crew clears away his tool kit and a can designed to hold ejector cartridges that are used to release the bombs from their racks. Ian Francis

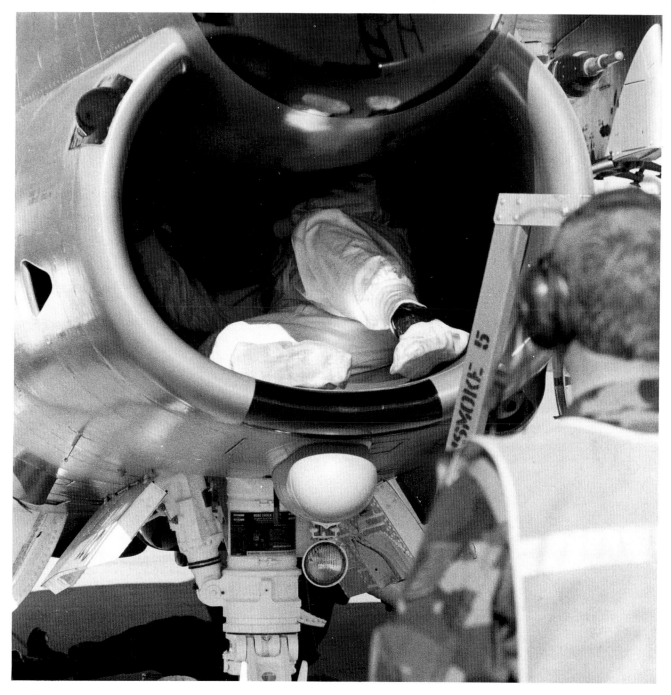

previous page
An A–7D from the 185th TFW is marshaled into the ICT loading area as this team's Loadeo event gets under way. Ian Francis

With the ICT supervisor looking on, this maintenance crew member goes down the throat of an A–7D to check the engine for any damage. White coveralls are worn over his BDU uniform to guard against anything dropping from his pockets while inside the intake. Ian Francis

Surrounded by munitions judges, this load crew chief gives a pretask briefing to his crew prior to starting the load on the A-7D in the background. Ian Francis

next page
The intense concentration needed for the Gunsmoke Loadeo events is shown on the face of this load crew chief as he signals the jammer driver to move in under an inert Mk 82. The nylon tiedown straps used to hold the bombs in their chocks during transport have been removed and the bomb has been pushed out onto extender rails, allowing the jammer table to move under it for pickup. The bomb will rest on the four rollers installed on the hydraulic table at the front of the lift arms; the four hydraulic control valves used to position the jammer table are clearly shown in this view. The gray strap next to the tool holder on this crew chief's belt has a hook-and-loop fastener strip down the center and is used to secure his ear defenders when they're not being worn. John Sheehan

Plenty of support from the rest of the Gunsmoke team in the bleachers during one of the Loadeo events. Teamwork is the key to success at Gunsmoke, and everybody on the team turns out for each *event to show support and provide that extra bit of encouragement that may make the difference in winning.* John Sheehan

Ready for the third Mk 82 on this A-10A, the load crew positions the bomb under the center station of the triple ejector rack. TSgt. Jose Lopez, Jr., AAVS

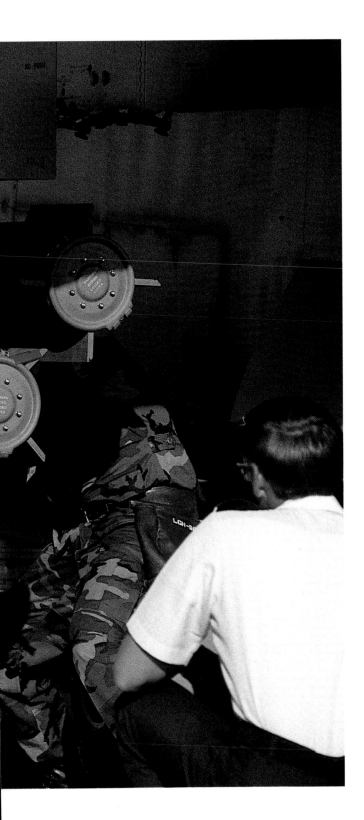

Loadeo action as the load crew completes the load of their third 500 lb. bomb on the triple ejector rack of an A-7D. A Gunsmoke weapons judge is close to the action, observing the crew as the jammer driver is signaled to back away from the aircraft. John Sheehan

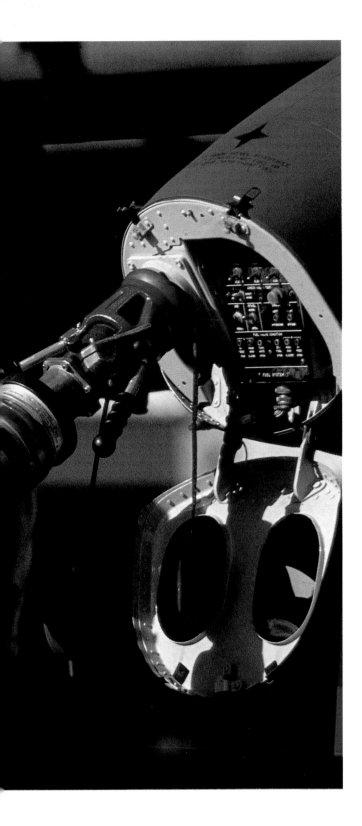

This A-10A crew chief gives the go-ahead to the fuel truck operator as he prepares to fuel the aircraft during an integrated combat turnaround (ICT) exercise at Gunsmoke 1987. The design of the A-10 places the fuel receptacle where it's easily accessible and at a comfortable working height, a real improvement over some earlier tactical aircraft. TSgt. Jose Lopez, Jr., AAVS

Gunsmoke Loadeo events can be decided by a small margin, and this load crew is taking no chances. The munitions judges will check every piece of paperwork after the load to ensure it was properly filled out—no crew wants to lose points because of an error in the forms. Ian Francis

An A-7D from the 185th TFG is loaded with three inert Mk 82 bombs at the completion of one of the team's Loadeo events. The pin inserted into the weapons pylon is a safety device designed to prevent the pylon bomb rack from inadvertently opening and dumping 1,500 pounds of bombs and a TER on some unsuspecting soul's toes. This aircraft also carries an Air Combat Maneuvering Instrumentation (ACMI) pod on the port fuselage AIM-9 missile rail. John Sheehan

This F-4E is equipped with TISEO, an acronym standing for Target Identification System, Electro-Optical. Ian Francis

Chapter 9

The Maintenance Game

The second half of the Gunsmoke equation belongs to the maintenance troops: the airplane general (APG) folks, or the nosepickers, as they're occasionally called. There's no way a team can make it at Gunsmoke with airplanes that break, and the pilots and WSOs know that it's the maintainers that make it possible for them to put the bombs and bullets where they need to be, on time. Any good Air Force outfit can fly jets, but the teams at Nellis can *really* fly

Not a Japanese exchange pilot, but the nametag worn by pilots of the 432nd TFW, Misawa AB, Japan. John Sheehan

Preparing for an early morning go, an F-4E crew chief gives the canopies a final touch-up prior to the crew's arrival. Gunsmoke puts the pressure on the ground crews to keep their aircraft nearly spotless, and most succeed. John Sheehan

them, as Maj. Gen. Billy G. McCoy explained: "Scheduling effectiveness—100 percent; air aborts—zero; non-effective sorties—zero; 466 sorties flown with 464 having been scheduled. We could have asked for no better."

Granted, this is a hand-picked group of professionals from some of the best flying units throughout the Air Force, but that's a flying record any tactical flying organization would be proud of.

The maintenance task starts early, well before the teams arrive at Nellis, when the aircraft are selected for Gunsmoke. Each jet is continually tweaked and massaged until it is flying as well as it is capable of—no "pigs" on a Gunsmoke team. Once the airplanes are up to speed, the pilots and WSOs take them on to the ranges at home station and put them through their paces. Any small problems can be fixed, but a major glitch with a jet is solved by replacing it and pressing on. Each team is absolutely confident in those airplanes when they depart for Nellis, and the maintenance crews work the airplanes daily to maintain that extra level of performance.

It takes a strong sense of trust and cooperation among all of the team members to make a success of the competition. Because each team is allowed to bring only forty specialists to support five aircraft, the large number of specialists normally found on the flightline is not available to respond to aircraft problems. A successful team has spent the months prior to the meet making sure that each maintenance member is qualified to work in several different positions, as called for. An engine specialist may be part of an ICT team, while an avionics repair technician doubles as part of the end-of-runway crew. During Gunsmoke, it's all part of the day's work and the troops realize the unique opportunity they have to learn what the other members of their team do for a living day-to-day. An A-10A maintainer put it like this: "You get a chance to show what you can do, competition; something different from home station. You do a variety of things in different jobs. You get to understand what goes on with other AFSCs (Air Force Specialty Code) and take it back to the AMU (Aircraft Maintenance Unit) and explain it to the other troops."

Sometimes it's not what you do, but how you do it, that makes the difference. Take the ICT, for example. Although each team brings their own maintenance crew to Gunsmoke, the fuel truck and its operator used during the ICT come from the local POL (petroleum, oil and lubricants) shop. These people haven't trained with the team, aren't a part of the team and have no vested interest in seeing a given team do well. This is where some of the skills that aren't taught in Air Force PME (Professional Military Education) classes come in. As one crew chief explained: "You have to brief 'em real, real good. You have to talk to the fuel truck driver and convince them to help out. When it's over, they might have a brand new patch to put on their jacket or for their collection."

Or maybe a brand-new case of beer in the trunk of their car. Although the ICT technical order specifies a range of fuel pressure to be used during fueling, if the driver bumps the pressure up a few pounds he can shave a few minutes off of the overall ICT time, and it's certainly worth a little "encouragement" on the part of the teams.

While aircraft performance is the main concern at Gunsmoke, how the aircraft look also plays a big part in the way each team is perceived by the judges. It's the old cliche about first impressions counting, and it's a way of life in the Air Force. With the competition as keen as it is here, the level of effort required to keep the aircraft looking good is considerably higher than it would be at home station. Aircraft paint has been touched up where necessary (up to 100 percent repaint, in some cases) and the ground crews seem to spend most of their time poring over each bird from nose to tail, cleaning up spills and leaks, wiping down landing gear struts and polishing canopies endlessly. After each day's flying ends, the cycle starts all over again.

Glitches happen, and then it's up to the specialists to talk with the pilot, pin down his problem with the airplane and then start tearing into the jet to isolate the malfunction and fix it—fast. Although there were maintenance problems among a few of the team aircraft, the flying statistics speak for themselves. This is one year when none of the spare pilots was called on to pull it out of the fire for a team aircraft that aborted.

While they watch for ways to stretch, if not bend, the rules, the maintenance members of the team are well aware of the rules that can cost them points in the overall maintenance scoring. In aircraft appearance, a leak or corrosion costs 30 points; a technical data violation or lack of foreign object control means a 70 point penalty; and a ground abort or hung ordnance will take 100 points away from their score. Any problems with work area cleanliness, haircuts or the appearance of their uniforms can cost them from 20 to 30 points—to be on the safe side, one group of maintainers shaved off their mustaches, every one of them. All of this makes for some pretty tense moments on the line as the maintenance technicians work to keep each aircraft at its peak, while the maintenance judges look for the slightest deviation from the books.

A stack of infrared decoy flares sits behind the main gear tire of an A-10A prior to loading. The maintenance crew member is wiping down the wheelwell to remove any minor hydraulic fluid leaks. Ian Francis

"It's kinda like getting stuck in the living room with your date's parents," in the words of one crew chief.

Maximum possible points in the maintenance competition are 1,000 for each of the six team missions, or a total of 6,000 points. At least one team, the 343rd TFW from Eilson AFB, Alaska, had a 1,000 point day. The overall maintenance award was won by the 944th TFG from Luke AFB, Arizona, with 5,991 points.

Continuous checks are one of the keys to success at Gunsmoke. This maintenance crew member examines one of his A-10A's turbofan engines. The white covers on the bottom of his boots help to prevent damage to the aircraft paint. The small antenna just visible on the rear fuselage is part of the Radar Homing and Warning (RHAW) system, designed to let the pilot know when he's being tracked by enemy radar. Ian Francis

next page
Ground crew members clean off their A-10A, including a wipe-down of the nose gear strut. Ian Francis

Two maintenance crew members find some shade under the wing of this Phantom II as they check out the aircraft maintenance forms. The TER on the pylon has been loaded with a BDU 33 practice bomb on each of its three stations. The red "remove before flight" streamers are attached to safety pins installed in each bomb rack of the TER. Ian Francis

This Gunsmoke maintenance judge takes notes as he inspects an F-4E assigned to the 4th TFW, Seymour Johnson AFB, North Carolina. A pair of F-16s head for the range in the background. TSgt. Jose Lopez, Jr., AAVS

PLOSIVE CHARGES
LADDER T
BE HELD
THE STOWE
POSITIO
BEFORE
CLOSING
DOOR
NTROL INTERCOM
DDER RELEASE

previous page
Another artistic touch on an A–10A, this one from the 930th TFG, Grissom AFB, Indiana. John Sheehan

An F-16 waits for crew arrival with the canopy raised in the morning sun. John Sheehan

Chapter 10

Behind the Scenes

Throughout Gunsmoke, the events are covered by live television pictures relayed from each range. Past meets featured pictures only, with no narration, but the most recent meet added a live commentator to provide information on each team's progress and the success of each pilot as they made their passes. Television coverage is remarkably good, coming from several cameras fitted with telephoto lenses and mounted on moveable platforms located near the range towers.

The camera operators, employed by Ford Aerospace under contract to the Air Force, track each jet as it enters the range and makes its run to the target. With a little practice it's possible to pick out the BDU 33 practice bombs as they leave the TER racks and track them down to the tank. Impact on the target is clearly visible on the television screens located in the Red Flag building and in the team hangars adjacent to the Gunsmoke ramp. As each aircraft makes a pass, its call sign and unit are superimposed over the picture, leaving no doubt as to who gets credit for the pass.

Television coverage has expanded to the point that it is carried on the Nellis AFB cable TV system, available in base housing and in the Base Exchange.

Along with the coverage from the range events, the television cameras are on the scene to record the details of each team's two Loadeo events. Specialists from the Air Force Audiovisual Service, headquartered at Norton AFB, California, spend each afternoon on the ramp, alongside the Gunsmoke teams, as they hustle from one side of an ICT to the other looking for the best view of the action. It makes for a long, hot day but the TV pictures serve to show the other face of Gunsmoke, the weapons loading teams that are essential to the Air Force mission—to fly, fight and win. Or to put it in the words of the load toads and BB stackers, "Without munitions, it's just another unscheduled airline."

In the end, like everything the Air Force does well, it's the people and not the machines that make it happen. No one could use fear or bribes to coax from people the amount of hard work and dedication displayed by the Gunsmoke teams. The fact that they work as hard and long as they do in the hunt for the top spots in the competition comes from one of the most amazing aspects of the Air Force way of life—a long tradition of professionalism and sacrifice. It's the same sense of duty that finds load crews on a wet and windy flightline at 3:00 A.M., soaking wet and freezing, but unwilling to hang it up until the last bomb is on the jet. And in spite of what you may have read in the press, it takes more than a leather jacket and flight pay to convince anyone in the flying game that the long hours, family hardships and the loss of good friends along the way are worth the sacrifices called for.

Gunsmoke is *people*. Team after team put that point across, sometimes in different words, but always the same thought—the people on our team are what make us competitive. Virtually all of the team members, from pilots, maintenance troops and public affairs officers to the load crew, are there because they want to be and they want the chance to show their stuff and be judged by their peers. In the words of one aircraft maintenance specialist, "The competition is indeed the Olympics of the Air Force." That attitude is reflected in the actions of everyone on the team as the meet progresses.

Along with the spirit of competition that pervades the Gunsmoke ramp, there's a lot of cooperation as well. A feeling that you owe it to the other teams to help them out when they have a problem, so each team has an equal chance at winning. "We deserve to see everybody do the best they can," said an F-16 driver. "We want to beat them fair and square."

This may be a matter of passing along some information on wind conditions on the range, or a suggestion on how to correct a problem with one of the aircraft. In another case, it's an offer to lend some aircraft parts to keep another team's jets flying. "We're all fighter pilots. Everybody cooperates, so the performances are the best they can be," said one pilot.

As another pilot put it: "We're more alike than not. If situations were changed, and we were stationed somewhere together, we'd probably be close friends with a lot of these guys."

There are a lot of sacrifices on the long road to Gunsmoke. Not just the extra time and effort the teams put in, but the effect all of that has on their personal lives. You can't make the concerted effort it takes to win something as highly competitive as Gunsmoke without a tremendous level of support from the folks at home. One airman on the 3rd TFW team put in a call to home as soon as the aircraft appearance judges had finished their inspection of the team's twenty-year-old F-4Es. That's when his wife told him that she had her own problems back in the Philippines to deal with, but hadn't said anything until the judging was over, so he wouldn't worry.

Another Air National Guard team brought an administrative specialist with them to Nellis who saw her job as something more than just pushing papers. Although it was her first Gunsmoke meet, she made it her business to find

The distinctive sharksteeth paint scheme on the nose of these A-10As from the 23rd TFW, England AFB, Louisiana, sets them apart from their gray and green sister ships assigned to other wings.

The small pylon mounted on the starboard side of the fuselage is designed to hold a Pave Penny laser pod. Ian Francis

Live television transmission from one of the Nellis ranges shows an F-4E of the 924th TFG, Bergstrom AFB, Texas, doing warp 8 on his run into the target. "Bucko" was the call sign used by the 924th *for Gunsmoke, and this is the team's number four aircraft. Live commentary accompanies the TV pictures which are provided to the Nellis cable TV system.* John Sheehan

her way around Nellis and take care of situations that would have kept the rest of the team from concentrating on their jobs. Because Gunsmoke begins just after the start of the USAF's new fiscal year, her team was not given advance per diem payments for the trip to Nellis. She made it her business to collect each individual's TDY (temporary duty) orders, get the necessary paperwork done and then handcarry the requests for payment to the base finance office. She picked up the checks the following day, and then dropped by the Nellis Base Exchange to ensure that the team members could cash their checks there. It may not sound like much, but to someone thousands of miles

from home with a thin wallet, that travel pay looks awfully good. Oh, yes—in between scrounging a coffeepot for the team's maintenance hangar and helping out with cleaning up the airplanes, she also made a 6:30 A.M. run to the local convenience store to pick up a bottle of red nail polish. Not for herself, but for some last-minute touch-up on the team's jets.

Then there's the three-man load crew from the South Carolina Guard that made a 2,300 mile trip from Seymour-Johnson ANGB to Nellis in a pickup truck. Why? "We just wanted to see the sights," one crew member commented. But that's another story.

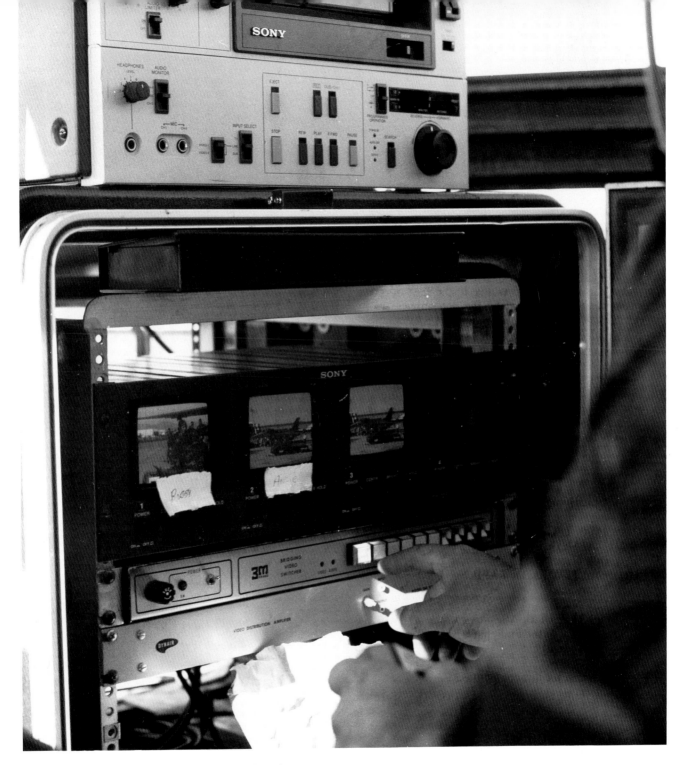

This truck-mounted "mini control center" is used to select camera shots as the unit director orchestrates live TV coverage of a Gunsmoke ICT event. John Sheehan

Chapter 11

And the Winners Are . . .

The results of this Gunsmoke meet are in and they confirm a clean sweep for the F–16 teams. In the face of some tough competition presented by the determined, experienced professionals from throughout the USAF Tactical Air Forces, the General Dynamics Fighting Falcon has performed as predicted, taking the top spot in each of the flying events.

Capt. Pat Shay from the 944th TFG, Luke AFB, Arizona, took the overall Top Gun award with an impressive score of 2,399.5 points out of the possible 2,500. The runners up in second through sixth positions were also flying the F–16, which is a clear indication not only of their skills but of the solid capabilities of that aircraft.

The top three non-F–16 teams were:

Aircraft type	Unit/Home base	Total points
A–7D	150th TFG Kirtland AFB, New Mexico (6th place)	9,052.5
A–10A	23rd TFW England AFB, Louisiana (8th place)	8,763.5
F–4E	3rd TFW Clark AB, Republic of the Philippines (11th place)	8,367.0

The top five teams for this competition were:

Place	Unit/Home base	Aircraft type	Total points
1	169th TFG McEntire ANGB, SC	F–16	9,313.5
2	944th TFG Luke AFB, AZ	F–16	9,254.0
3	432nd TFW Misawa AB, Japan	F–16	9,157.0
4	388th TFW Hill AFB, UT	F–16	9,127.5
5	347th TFW Moody AFB, GA	F–16	9,091.0

Coming in a mere 59 points back from the Swampfoxes of the 169th was the newest F–16 team in the competition, the 944th assigned to Luke AFB, Arizona. In addition to one team member taking the honors as Top Gun, the 944th swept the two maintenance categories, placing first in the aircraft maintenance and aircraft loading standings with 5,991 points and 2,910 points respectively.

Aircraft maintenance category winners were:

Aircraft type	Unit/Home base	Total points
A–10A	930th TFG Grissom AFB, Indiana (2nd place, overall)	5,984.0
A–7D	185th TFG Sioux City ANGB, Iowa (6th place overall)	5,963.0
F–4E	3rd TFW Clark AB, Republic of the Philippines (13th place overall)	5,909.0

Top spots in the aircraft loading competition were won by:

Aircraft type	Unit/Home base	Total points
A–10A	81st TFW RAF Bentwaters, England (3rd place, overall)	2,790.0

Aircraft type	Unit/Home base	Total points
F-4E	3rd TFW Clark AB, Republic of the Philippines (5th place, overall)	2,740.0
A-7D	150th TFG Kirtland AFB, New Mexico (8th place, overall)	2,700.0

The 169th TFG's third trip to Gunsmoke proved to be the one that made it all worthwhile. The Swampfoxes fielded a team comprised of two Air National Guard "full-timers," two pilots who fly for commercial airlines and pull part-time guard duty, and the spare pilot who was waiting for a job with the airlines. The four primary pilots were competitors in Gunsmoke 1987, and their experience paid off handsomely as the team made their steady climb to the top after a slow start during the first few days of the meet.

At the end of the Profile I bombing and strafing events the 169th had dropped from third place and finished with a lock on fifth place, scoring 2,924.5 points. However, the team's experience level paid off. "Everybody kept cool," said Maj. George "Jet" Jernigan, the team leader. "It would have been easy to throw in the towel, but nobody did."

As predicted, the top team at Gunsmoke was decided in the two Profile III rides. By the time the team from South Carolina was ready for their second nav-attack mission, it boiled down to their number two pilot needing a great ride if the team was going to take home the trophy. His F-16 had been doing well up to that point. "When he got to the flightline, his crewchief briefed him on a problem with one of the hydraulic actuators that control the engine nozzle. It put the airplane out of commission and would cost the team 40 points if we took a ground abort," said Jernigan. "It's normally an hour to an hour and a half job to fix. We sent the pilot down to preflight the spare aircraft, and our people started swarming all over his airplane. They were cool and calm, working like machines. Before he had the spare preflighted, they came down and told him his jet was ready—they'd changed the actuator in 18 minutes."

With that level of support, how can you lose? The number two pilot finished his second Profile III flight with 880 out of a possible 900 points, and that clinched the top team award for the 169th.

Jernigan continued: "We had a good contingency plan and good aircraft; we were shooting for a faultless performance in all areas. We did have some unforeseen maintenance problems crop up that we hadn't expected. Aircraft 288 had been hot before we got to Nellis, but during two of the Profile I passes all the HUD symbology disappeared—it turned out to be a wiring problem and we had to use the spare aircraft, which was not that good. Another jet had flown 100 sorties with no problems, but it hung up an entire TER at Nellis."

A pair of Gunsmoke pilots talk over the day's events and check out the scoreboard. Scores are posted daily as the events are flown, and while the top two or three teams won't change, the rest of the pack moves up and down in the points daily total. John Sheehan

"The quality of our people and their preparation made the difference. The level of expertise in the Guard saved the day—we won on the strength of our people," Jernigan added.

The team members felt that the level of competition had not been as tough in 1987. All the teams were better prepared and had paid attention to the "lessons learned" from prior meets, picking up ways to tweak the jets and improve avionics performance. "We've got the most talented maintenance people in the world. They provide superb maintenance. Day in and day out, the aircraft work," said Jernigan.

In the Guard and Reserve units, a crew chief may stay with a jet for ten years—they take a lot of pride in it. The 169th in particular is proud of its family atmosphere. Jernigan related: "We've got a water volleyball team made up of crewchiefs—they call themselves the 'Cowpokers.' On my last flight the crewchief came on the interphone and broke the tension a little by saying, 'Have a good flight and we thank you very much for flying Cowpoker airlines.'"

F-16s of the 944th TFG, Luke AFB, Arizona. This Air Force Reserve unit was formed in 1987 and after a short two years with the F-16 was a top contender at Gunsmoke 89. The 944th team ran a strong second for the overall fighter unit award, but took first place honors for aircraft maintenance and weapons loading, as well as two individual awards; Capt. Pat Shay was named the meet's Top Gun, and SSgt. Joedy Pack was picked as the top aircraft crew chief. John Sheehan

Epilogue

As this book was being written, people in countries all across Eastern Europe were pouring into the streets to demand an end to the totalitarian governments that had ruled them since the end of World War II. To the amazement of the citizens of western democracies, the whole process took place within months, not decades, and with relatively little bloodshed. Suddenly, the terms "evil empire" and "Warsaw Pact forces" lost much of their power to inflame. With these dramatic changes in mind, it's difficult to give much credence to the scenario of a flight of A-10s taking on a column of T-72 tanks breaking out of East Germany and heading for the Fulda Gap. The vehicles that poured across the border were aging Trabants, stuffed to the headliners with citizens of the DDR looking for the good life in the west.

What does this all have to do with Gunsmoke? As fast as the governments fell in the east, the US Congress was demanding larger and larger reductions in the defense budget. It costs money to fly airplanes and buy the bombs and bullets for them—assuming the aircraft haven't been mothballed and the pilots and ground crews separated from the service in the name of economy. It's difficult to predict what the final size and composition of the Air Force will be until all of the votes are in, but it seems likely that it will be a much smaller force operating on a lot fewer dollars. And that means potentially less support for high-cost operations such as Gunsmoke and its sister event, William Tell.

If Gunsmoke does continue, some major changes are likely. It's almost certain that the F-4s will be gone soon, perhaps to be replaced by the F-15E Strike Eagle. If and when that happens, we'll be in for some impressive flying and the boys in the Lawn Darts will be staying up late to figure out how to stay in the running. From all accounts, the Strike Eagle is a bomb-dropping fool.

At the same time, the future of the A-7D is in doubt. Although LTV (Ling, Temco and Vought) has placed great faith in the improved A-7 (designated the A-7F), there is not much hope that the dollars will be there to fund it if F-16s can be retired from the active force to replace the Corsairs of the Air National Guard. The A-10 community is in transition, being moved slowly from a dedicated role as ground attack aircraft to their new incarnation as OA-10s, eventually replacing OA-37s and OV-10s as FAC (Forward Air Control) aircraft. Whether anyone in the Congress is ready to put up the money for a fleet of ground attack F-16s (A-16s?) to replace the Warthogs remains to be seen.

Gunsmoke may continue in a reduced form, possibly with an increased interval of three or four years. If new capabilities are funded for existing aircraft, the individual events may be modified to allow increased use of these electronic systems, perhaps going as far as using laser or electro-optically guided munitions. If that happens, someone has cut the purse strings, because those items can run into big bucks (or as the old Congressional saw goes, "A million here, a million there, and pretty soon you're talking real money").

No matter what happens, keep in mind that the fighter community is a pretty resourceful bunch of folks. They brought Gunsmoke back after a nineteen-year break in the competition, and if there's a way to keep it going, they'll find it. Wish 'em luck!